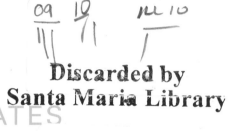

KITCHEN PLAYDATES

Easy Ideas for Entertaining That Include the Kids
70 Delicious Recipes ● Plus Menus, Activities, and 10 Playdates

By Lauren Bank Deen / Photographs by Tina Rupp

CHRONICLE BOOKS
SAN FRANCISCO

Library of Congress Cataloging-in-Publication Data available.

ISBN-10: 0-8118-5539-2
ISBN-13: 978-0-8118-5539-6

. . . .

Manufactured in China.

Design and typesetting by NOON.
Prop styling by Deborah Williams.
Food styling by Toni Brogan.

. . . .

Distributed in Canada by Raincoast Books
9050 Shaughnessy Street
Vancouver, British Columbia V6P 6E5

10 9 8 7 6 5 4 3 2 1

CHRONICLE BOOKS LLC
680 Second Street
San Francisco, California 94107
www.chroniclebooks.com

TABLE OF CONTENTS

CHAPTER 1 | **PLAYDATES**

Modern and Easy Food for Busy Parents and Kids

Ah, family life. I'd be lying if I said I didn't miss the old days just a little bit: drinks on a Saturday night at some great new lounge followed by dinner at the fabulous place just reviewed in Wednesday's *New York Times*. Maybe it's a friend's restaurant, where my guests and I are treated like royalty, course after delicious course, lots of provocative adult conversation, and barely a thought of the time.

Feels like a whole other lifetime. Nowadays, I can't even look at that tempting lychee panna cotta without calculating whether it's going to be worth the extra hour of babysitting it will cost me to linger for dessert. A nightcap? Not a chance.

The arrival of my children changed an aspect of my life that I was pretty happy with: the opportunity for social spontaneity, including the occasional nightcap or a long Sunday brunch at a restaurant. Of course my husband, Anthony, and I are absolutely crazy about our kids, Mathias and Natasha, and can't imagine life without them. But we have both had a little pang for certain aspects of the way things were.

Family life is chaotic—there's just no way around it. So, I decided, why not embrace it? I'm a problem solver by trade and temperament; how hard could it be to do the family thing and see friends, too? Through a little trial and error I found that I didn't have to give up my former life, just reinvent it a little.

My experience gained from cooking school and years as a caterer were a help. Since I now make my living producing lifestyle TV for everyone from Martha Stewart to the Food Network, I took the organizing skills I used on the job and tackled the get-togethers, so there's no sweat, and fewer tears. What I do at home isn't a perfect television segment. It's messy. It's real. My "staff" is prone to giggle fits. And that's the charm.

Practicality with style has become my signature. Although I have worked with some of the world's top chefs as the first sous chef at the Food Network and as a TV producer, my experience as a mother has taught me to leave complicated restaurant cooking to the pros. My skill is in taking the tricks and techniques I've seen in their kitchens and backstage on the set and translating them so they make sense to the home cook. The result is delectable food that isn't a pain to prepare and doesn't require a staff of highly skilled assistants. I've included all the little helpful details that often get lost in translation—like using muffin tins for individual desserts instead of fumbling with ramekins, or lining a cake pan with buttered foil and sticking it on a sheet pan when you can't find the bottom because the kids are using it as a drum.

One other thing you should know about me: I like to get involved in my friends' lives. Not in a nosy way, just in an "I'm here to help" way. I hate that so few of them feel comfortable cooking, and that the ones who used to cook are giving it up because of time pressures. I've made myself available to them, and they've taken me up on my offers. I've even been known to hold the occasional impromptu weekend lesson to help a friend figure out everything from baking a chocolate cake to tackling the Thanksgiving turkey. Answering their questions and leading those Sunday afternoon how-to sessions became the beginnings of *Kitchen Playdates*.

So what exactly is a kitchen playdate? It's a playdate that includes the grown-ups, complete with great food and if you're up for it, a cooking project with the kids. I realized that many of the old entertaining rules are outdated and don't reflect the way we really live now. With such busy weeks, we want to see our friends and our kids. Now Saturday night includes everyone; we don't send the kids to bed and get a sitter. Granted, things start a bit earlier, but it's just as much fun. I invite the parents and their kids over at three so we can all relax and enjoy each other before the young ones melt down. When you entertain other families, you can have everything prepared beforehand, or ask friends to pitch in. You can cook with the kids or without. There are suggestions for tasks that are child appropriate, and the rest is up to you, depending on your schedule and state of mind and the kids' moods and ages.

These are get-togethers you actually get to attend. The kids help, and the adults help. When you want a little time with just the adults, send the kids into the other room to snap beans, twist pretzels out of pizza dough, or do an art project. It's a fresh change from stressed-out entertaining or ordering in the same old Chinese food.

As far as I'm concerned the words "perfect" and "parent" just don't go together. And there's nothing wrong with that. These informal get-togethers with friends and family are low stress and are meant to be loosey-goosey. You won't need crazy gadgets. You won't be asked to perform knife skills worthy of the Japanese steak house. You don't even have to make all this food from scratch. No reason you can't use a roast chicken from the deli counter to simplify things—just serve it with a killer side dish like Sweet Potato Salad with Lime and Ancho (page 96). Your guests won't hold it against you. Flexibility is one of the qualities you need most when you're a parent. The same applies here. I've organized things so you can make your events as casual or refined as you want them to be.

These recipes are meant to be mixed and matched, and come with suggestions for items you can buy ready-made to reduce the workload. Most can be halved easily, or doubled. The point is to revel in your little imperfect bit of paradise, not to *tend* to the party, but *attend* the party and enjoy your friends and family. The recipes are simple yet stylish, full of easy-to-find ingredients with a global range that reflects the ethnic markets, restaurants, and neighborhoods I've been lucky enough to live near and visit. I've test-driven and adapted these dishes so they are sophisticated in spirit, yet firmly grounded in the reality that comes with being a busy parent. You're not sacrificing a thing. That was the firm rule. So good-bye intricate latticework atop my signature linzertorte. It's updated with a simple polka-dot pattern that the kids can do with cookie cutters (page 119). The new recipe is speedier, and looks fabulous and modern. Plus there's dough leftover that we can freeze to make cookies the next time the playground is rained out. It's all about flexibility and fun, not fuss.

There are no hard-and-fast rules to follow, and you will have plenty of chances to relax with good food, family, and friends. Ready to schedule your first playdate?

CHAPTER 2 | **COOKING WITH KIDS**

Children need to be comfortable in the kitchen, to understand real food and the sense of community that the best casual entertaining inspires. So make them a part of the process. The importance of their experiences in the kitchen can be measured in so many ways.

Kids can learn from almost anything that goes right or wrong in the kitchen. Cooking really helps teach discipline and patience. You can't skip any steps: If you don't butter the pan well, the cake will stick. You must stir the Lime Curd (page 131) constantly, or you will have scrambled eggs.

The kitchen is really the world writ small, if you think about it. All the things you learn there can be applied to your life away from the stove, too. This is especially true for kids. Cooking teaches math through all the weighing, measuring, sorting, and combining. It's also a great big ongoing science project. They learn what heat and leavening do to cookie dough, and how a whisk and a cold metal bowl transform heavy cream. A kitchen playdate also helps children build motor skills while they roll and punch out cookies or shell peas.

Cooking with kids gives them a greater sense of ownership over what goes into their bodies. They'll know how much sugar or fat goes into their favorite foods, and see and taste the difference between homemade and store-bought. These experiences will help them make better nutritional choices throughout their lives.

Welcoming your kids into the kitchen is also a great way to let them experience the pride of creation, the challenge of tackling a recipe, and the confidence success builds. Sure, the frustration that comes with a fallen soufflé also lurks in the kitchen, but even the lessons learned from an all-out culinary disaster are golden. Recipes build reading skills, while plate presentation scratches their itch for design. All five of a child's developing senses are tickled and challenged by time spent cooking with a parent, which brings us to the best reason to throw a kitchen playdate: spending time with your kids. Quality time like this isn't easy to come by.

The "Kids in the Kitchen" note found below each recipe provides suggested steps and tasks that are best suited for children. (While there is rarely a time that the kitchen pyrotechnics get too dangerous, there is also one "Kids Out of the Kitchen" safety note on page 142.)

The good news is that just about every child is happy to dig his or her hands into a lump of dough, try a cool tool, and help decorate anything and everything in sight. That can also be the bad news when you're in a rush or tired. So my biggest rule, really the only rule outside of safety issues, is know your mood and assign appropriate tasks that reflect that. If you have the time, take as long as you need to give everyone a chance to get the most out of the experience. If you're crunched, quickly spot the task that will keep the small hands busy, and avoid the one that will try your patience.

General Safety Rules

- Remind kids to wash their hands before handling food.

- Make sure they roll up their sleeves; long hair should be pulled back.

- Understand that knives are not toys, and while they're a cool tool, they can also cut fingers.

- Stoves are for grown-ups or older children; the burners and oven get very hot and can cause painful injuries.

- Equipment can be dangerous: Outlets should not be touched. Cords should be neatly coiled or tied up so as not to trip anyone. Remind kids to keep fingers out of standing mixers. Blenders have sharp blades in the bottom of the cup, and food processor blades are even sharper.

- Food safety is important, too. Keep things at their proper temperatures. Time can get away from you when kids are in the kitchen, so make sure perishables stay in the refrigerator until you need them. Hands and cutting boards need to be carefully washed after touching raw poultry, meat, or eggs.

Getting Started

- Briefly explain the dish and read the recipe ingredients and steps to the kids before you begin.

- Have the kids help gather any equipment you need before starting so you're not scrambling while cooking.

- Set up your station like they do at a restaurant or on the Food Network. Put a wet towel under the cutting board to reduce slippage. Set out your tools and a bowl for trash and trimmings. Have all ingredients—your *mise en place,* to use the correct kitchen jargon—on a nearby tray or easily accessible.

- Divide or share prep tasks such as washing, tearing, mixing, grating, and chopping, depending on the age of the children. Make sure to assign the right tools for little hands.

- When you show kids how to measure, explain the tools. But also teach them how to be self-reliant and use their eyes to help them develop a sense of how much, say, a tablespoon is. As a result, younger children will be less likely to grab the measuring spoons from one another. Measure out salt or sugar into your palm, using each of the measuring spoons, one at a time, to see what ¼ teaspoon really looks like compared to 1 tablespoon.

- Don't worry about the mess. Teach kids to be neat, but don't get too hyper about drips and dribbles. It will chip away at their confidence and pride.

- Reset your adult time clock. Things, as any parent knows, take longer when there are small, eager hands involved. So make sure you have added extra time so that you don't feel pressure and then get tense. I usually look at the menu and carve out either an entire recipe or parts of a few recipes so that we have a good time, and cooking doesn't become a battle of wills.

○ Keep your sense of humor and let go of your desire for perfection—this is supposed to be fun, after all!

○ Have some snacks along the way—kids of almost any age get impatient and want to eat what you're making before you've cooked it.

○ Know your child. Natasha will want to be involved in every step and wash the dishes. Mathias, on the other hand, is really interested in the active moments, like cracking eggs or flipping the Stuffed French Toast (page 162), and then he's out of there.

○ Make age-appropriate choices. Keep the babies in the kitchen with you to get used to the sounds and smells. There are plenty of rubber spatulas, measuring cups, and other safe kitchen toys to keep them happy. When they are on solid food, let them taste appropriate foods and make a mess. Toddlers are happy to help and have their own jobs. By three they can measure, stir, cut with a plastic knife, and have their own set of tools and aprons. Their attention spans and patience levels are still a bit short, and so make sure the tasks are short, too, and achievable. Coach them along. By seven or so, or whenever they begin to read, they can look over the recipe, and assign the younger kids tasks (under adult supervision). They can also use small knives and handle some tools, like can openers, graters, mixers, and blenders. Some older kids may be ready to use the stove and food processor. It's tricky to determine exactly when, and the grown-ups should evaluate each child individually. Safety first, and appropriate instructions and supervision are key.

○ Remember to work safely yourself, and avoid risky shortcuts. Children learn from watching. If you bend too close to the mixer, or toss the food processor blade into soapy water where someone could get cut by it, they will do the same.

○ Be creative. Tell stories to keep kids engaged. If it's a family recipe, tell them its personal history. If it's from another country or a place they have visited or studied, put it into context for them.

○ Include the science and math. I keep my laptop nearby. While I'm a trained cook, I don't know the reason for every culinary reaction, so we look it up online.

○ Add music if it won't be too distracting. I admit it, I'm a goofball and I like to match the music to the menu. I rely on humor or my horrid singing voice and awkward dancing to get us out of those "Mommy, he peeled my potato" moments. Anything from OutKast to the theme from the play *Pippin* stops the fighting fairly quickly!

○ Start a family cookbook. Create new recipes, transcribe your grandmother's recipes, and find favorites on the Web. Take pictures of your finished dishes and parties and print out a little cookbook for holiday presents.

Kids at the Table

Involving kids in preparing meals means more than cooking. When you have the chance, teach your children to be aware of their environment. Explain why you have flowers at the table, or even just a colorful arrangement of fruit in a bowl. Point out the differences between thick, hand-thrown pottery mugs and translucent china. In the suggested playdate parties scattered throughout the book, there are great ideas for table-related projects—decorating placemats, personalizing teacups, making centerpieces, and of course setting the table. The more involved the kids are in preparing for the meal, the more they seem to respect and understand the need for good table manners.

A Note on Nutrition

I am not a nutritionist, but fortunately my brother-in-law, Dr. Darwin Deen, is! Darwin winced at first and later rejoiced through seventeen years of my family meals. I say "wince" because the amount of heavy cream I used during my Francophile cooking school days had him worrying for my husband's heart. Though family pride leads me to suggest Darwin's book *Nutrition for Life*, which he coauthored with Dr. Lisa Hark, there are a lot of great family-friendly nutrition and diet books and Web sites out there to help you navigate through the confusing array of information and avoid fad diets. See the Sources on page 173. Your pediatrician or personal doctor should be able to recommend a good book and give you a sense of what your family should be eating.

Kitchen Playdates reflects what I think is a healthy balance of vegetables, fruit, and protein-rich food, with the occasional indulgence—a rich Sunday baked pasta, or a sugary sweet birthday cake. Simply roasting or occasionally grilling fish or chicken and accenting the dish with a bright salsa or relish is my way of sneaking in veggies. A sprinkle of grated cheese ends a rebellion against green vegetables, too.

The USDA's recommended Five a Day for Better Health Program (at least five daily servings of fruits, legumes, and vegetables) is a challenge for any parent, but it's important for your children's health. Try to increase the amount of fruits and vegetables they eat by letting them choose some at the market, or grow them. Try buying the oddest vegetables that you can find, such as a knobby celery root or blood orange. Switch to multigrain breads, waffles, and pancake mixes, and cook grains instead of plain pasta. It's critical to avoid trans fats, now clearly labeled, and monitor the amount of fatty, sweet, processed, and fried junk food your kids eat. I find it becomes less of a battle the more time they spend around real food. They notice the difference in quality in homemade food, especially if they make it themselves.

Cooking in the Classroom

Once a month I head over to my son's kindergarten class at the local public school to share a recipe that is somehow tied to what is going on in class, beyond the usual holiday baking. For example, we made cookie bear paws with slivered almonds for nails when they were studying bears, and Chocolate Play Dough (page 136) when they were discussing shapes. We have also played with baking soda and made yeast breads and healthy dips in science class.

Cooking with schoolkids is the most entertaining thing you can do. Their enthusiasm is intoxicating, the glorious mess is pretty much unparalleled, and their honest reactions range from bliss to disgust. You're a witness to so many important things that are going on at the same time—the recognition of flavors and sensations, the acquisition of new skills, and their consideration of mathematical and scientific principles. Kids also learn sharing, and patience. And all of this is capped by the sense of wonder that comes from watching corn muffins rise and the pride that accompanies a job well done.

Explore the options at your school. The New York City Board of Education's regional director heard about what I was doing in my son's classroom and asked me to expand the program schoolwide. You can be ambitious or keep your efforts small in scale. Work with the teachers, the PTA, or like-minded parents to create a program or just a yearly event that you can manage within your schedule. At my son's school, we're working on an international program that reflects the diverse ethnic backgrounds of the kids. Some events will take place during school hours and others in an after-school program. The teachers put together their first cookbook. We're also writing a grant to address healthier eating habits and fund a "lunchbox makeover" workshop for parents and kids.

I have outlined a program at www.kitchenplaydates.com. You can use some of the recipes from this book. Or consider inviting chefs to come to your kids' school to teach about fresh, local, healthy food. For information, visit www.spoonsacrossamerica.org. Research other schools that have started programs, like the Edible Schoolyard (pioneered by Alice Waters), or start your own. For example, my cousins have started a cooking lab, Jeff's Kitchen, in memory of local restaurateur Jeff Salaway at the Hayground School in Bridgehampton (www.hayground.org). Look into the program at Boston's Kids Can Cook, an urban middle school, after-school experience that teaches important life skills in a safe and nurturing environment through the art and science of cooking (www.kidscancook.org).

○ PAPER PLAYDATE ○

While the kitchens at Martha Stewart Television were a wonder to behold, nothing was more magical to me than the craft department: rows of tissue paper, perfectly folded in every color imaginable (and some created by layering different colors); bins of glues; rows of ribbons; and jars of buttons. For someone as craft-impaired as I am, it was a land of mystery and inspiration. I would hang around and beg the professional crafters to wrap my gifts while I watched, trying to soak up as much as I could. I've been a paper addict ever since, and I have as much tissue paper as Anthony will let me bring into the house, including rolls of cellophane and butcher paper.

I designed this playdate to clear out some of my paper stash and amuse the kids on a rainy day when the cousins were over. The main activity for the kids is assembling the packets of fish for Parchment-Baked Halibut with Shiitakes, Lemon, and Herbs (page 61). It's a healthy and "crafty" dish. Set everything up assembly-line style. First cut and oil the sheets of parchment or let older kids do this. Have plates with the fish, mushrooms, lemons, herbs, and seasonings down the center. Let the kids assemble the packets, as well as those of their parents, by twisting them into big bonbons. Throw them into the fridge, wash up, and move on to the paper party.

You can lay out a long plain tablecloth for everyone to decorate collage-style, let the kids do origami if you have the talent and patience, or cut out paper dinosaur dolls or snowflakes. There are great books on folding paper airplanes, too. You can also have the kids make paper cones to serve different colored sorbets for dessert.

MENU

- EDAMAME DIP (PAGE 41)
- ASIAN RICE-PAPER SUMMER ROLLS (STORE-BOUGHT)
- PARCHMENT-BAKED HALIBUT WITH SHIITAKES, LEMONS, AND HERBS (PAGE 61)
- ASIAN RADICCHIO SLAW (PAGE 99)
- HONEY AND LIME FRUIT SALAD (PAGE 121)
- SORBETS IN PAPER CONES

GEAR TO GET

This equipment list has been seriously test-driven beginning in my early cooking school days and ending with the latest show I've produced. I've played with all the kitchen toys that are out there. Martha's studio was a culinary kingdom—rows of gleaming pots and pans, and felt-lined drawers filled with every tool imaginable. For the Food Network trend show *What's Hot! What's Cool!* we were sent the wacky and the sublime—things like indoor s'more kits and silk woven tea bags. Here's what I think will really help you, whether you're in a hurry or want to play at your leisure. I've cut through the kitchen clutter to find the must-haves and discarded the dust collectors. For where to find everything, see the Sources on page 173.

RESTAURANT HALF-SHEET PANS (RIMMED BAKING SHEETS)

These are truly as indispensable as a sauté pan. I passed over an otherwise ideal refrigerator because it couldn't easily accommodate these pans. I use these 13-by-18-inch aluminum pans to roast cut-up chicken or vegetables. Millions of cookies have been baked on them. I've placed them under countless cakes and plastic zipped marinating bags, and I keep one in the oven at all times for warming everything from breakfast pancakes to take-out dinners.

As for why they need to fit in the fridge, you can't beat them for arranging hors d'oeuvres that can be made ahead and chilled, like Stuffed Dates (page 36). I also use them to organize the ingredients when I'm preparing a lot of different recipes for one party

or holiday meal. Buy at least three at a restaurant-supply store. And if they only sell them by the dozen, split them with a friend.

SCHIFF OFFSET SERRATED KNIFE

I'm primarily a Wüsthof girl, but my brother bought me this seven-inch beauty when I started cooking school. Eighteen years later, it's still the first knife that I reach for. It's a workhorse that easily slices through bread, tomatoes, and cheese. It also has the perfect angle and edge for chopping chocolate into fine shards for melting.

SILICONE WARE

Almost every baking pan has a silicone version. I use the flat mats for cookies, meringues, candied nuts, and even bacon. I've found heart-shaped muffin pans that I use for Panna Cotta (page 144), and for extra cake batter when I can't find the right size pan. I keep a few different sizes. My Baker's Dozen Eggs (page 155) and Sticky Toffee Pudding (page 140) fit in the standard size, and the Coconut Tartlets (page 135) nestle inside the minis for assembly-line ease. And I love the way the new silicone basting brushes never leave those stray hairs in your food.

PANS

I have pricey copper pans that I've shipped home from Dehillerin in France and cast-iron pans that I bought for a dollar at yard sales. I think the only way to buy a pan is to pick it up, handle it, and see how comfortable it is. Just make sure the manufacturer is reputable, which you can easily research

online. There are many well-made pans available at different price points. My favorites are the All-Clad stainless, Calphalon, and copper Dehillerin from France. For Dutch ovens, I like Le Creuset, Staub, and Lodge cast iron. Whenever possible, try to get ovenproof, stay-cool handles. Good pans are worth their money because they keep the heat evenly, the weight feels comfortable in the hand, and a good one will outlive you. I've inherited quite a few beauties from my grandmother, and they're going strong.

SPATULAS

Anthony is astonished at how many spatulas sit near the stove, and seem to spontaneously reproduce. Since I tend to be slightly klutzy, these are better versions of my busy and sometimes slippery hands.

OFFSET SPATULAS Having a few of these in different sizes can help you get out of a tricky spot. I find the tiny 4½-inch Ateco offset icing spatula can add a flourish or fix your frosting, and it will do a better job of coaxing a sticky cake or muffin from the pan than the usual butter or paring knife. Buy a few; they are inexpensive and they are perfect for little hands. (Which is why they tend to get lost.) The larger, traditional icing spatula from Ateco makes fast work of spreading frosting, cheeses, or dressings. Wüsthof makes a great spatula that costs a bit more, but I've had mine for seventeen years and I grab it all the time for flipping pancakes and scraping up pan drippings.

WIDE SILICONE SPATULAS I find these work really well for flipping omelets or transferring delicate fish fillets.

LARGE RUBBER SPOON OR SPATULA For the softest touch when folding egg whites for cakes and meringues.

WOODEN SPATULA I reach for a flat 3-inch version more often than the wooden spoons—it scrapes up all the yummy bits of a sauté for an instant pan sauce, and gets into all the corners.

MICROPLANE ZESTER

For fluffy, snowy Parmesan, citrus zest, nutmeg, and ginger. I even use this for garlic when I am too lazy to reach for a knife.

THE GADGET DRAWER

GRADUATED COOKIE CUTTERS These are sold in sets in different shapes—rings, squares, fluted, and hearts.

THERMOMETERS You need three, an oven thermometer to occasionally test your oven's calibration, an instant-read for checking the temperature of roasted meats, and a candy thermometer to test the temperature of oil for frying.

WINE OPENER I like the Screwpull or Rabbit, and my husband is partial to the waiter's, so we have both.

SUEDE POT HOLDERS

This is where my love of silicone ends. I find oven mitts clumsy, and the handy kitchen towels are usually a bit wet, and ends up conducting the heat instead of insulating me from it. Dean & DeLuca used to be the only place to find these, but I'm happy to say my local cookware shop now stocks them in a variety of colors. Suede pot holders are flexible, and can be thrown in the washing machine without deteriorating. They last forever.

PINT-SIZED GEAR

Children's hands sometimes require tools on a smaller scale, depending upon their age. I have found that many "child-sized" tools aren't that helpful in the end, but some make all the difference, reducing frustration and increasing self-confidence. It's often a case of trial and error. Below are the items I've found most useful.

OXO PEELER

SHAKER-STYLE ROLLING PIN

MINI SILICONE ROLLING PIN

SAFE SMALL STEP STOOL

PLASTIC KNIVES

SMALL CUTTING BOARD

WILTON'S PLASTIC OVERSIZED COOKIE CUTTERS

RUBBER TOOLS FOR TODDLERS

CHEF'S DUDS

My friend Rochelle Fleck's company, Chefwear, started the funky chef garb trend. They have adorable overalls, aprons, jackets, and hats for kids (see the Sources on page 173). A new dishtowel makes the perfect toddler apron once you sew on the ties.

SETTING THE SCENE

CREATE A PROP CLOSET

You may wonder: Why is it the tables in the glossy magazines never look like mine? Do I really need a closet filled with floral foam? Where do the wineglasses go? On all the shows I produce, we spend an enormous amount of time setting the tone and style of a table. While most of us don't have a rainbow of cloth napkins in our closets, a few well-chosen pieces add a touch of easy style.

Whether you live in a big house with an extra closet or are cozy in a snug apartment, designate a big drawer or bin for your tableware. You'll use your nice things more. If they aren't stashed away, you won't be inclined to save them for "company." Let's face it, that's akin to my great-grandmother's plastic-covered couch. My point is, buy it only if you will truly use it, and if you've bought it, enjoy it.

What to buy depends on your budget and storage space. I tend to collect basics from restaurant-supply stores and big box stores (like Pottery Barn and Crate & Barrel) that can do double duty: plain white coffee cups that can also contain crumbles or Panna Cotta (page 144), vases that can become carafes, and glasses that make nice votive holders. And forget the notion that things must be in matched sets. Breakage occurs, and mismatched tableware and dishes add charm and allow you to buy the odd, lone but gorgeous teacup on the sale table.

I also hunt down antique or more ornate touches such as vases, candlesticks, and funny little brass animals to add to the table so it isn't too plain. Oddly shaped platters

help add some graphic punch to a simply set table. Give the table an interesting dimension by adding height—cake stands for cheese, trifle bowls or martini glasses filled with Pickled Shrimp with Mango and Fennel (page 47).

Seek out things that are comfortable for kids. Smaller cups for little hands are adorable and seem to remind the kids that the table is a special place that deserves special behavior. (Make sure they aren't too precious.) We use the kids' initialed baby spoons, which they received as gifts, with the sugar bowl and salt cellar.

COVERING THE TABLE

The big stores always have sales on tablecloths and napkins. If you can hem, a few bolts of offbeat fabric can be a big gesture that changes the feel of a room rather quickly. I am pathetic with a needle and thread so I barter, making birthday cakes for a friend who whips up table runners. Sometimes I stock up on inexpensive tablecloths and fabric markers or paint and let the kids decorate while I finish cooking.

Remember, there are many ways to cover and decorate the table. Use the rolls of butcher paper from the kids' art supplies, and colored vellum squares for kid-friendly placemats. Children can tie old scarves onto the chairs and practice making bows. One little guy made wacky sailor's knots with napkins. It became a contest and stopped a lot of whining. A roll of ribbon can save the day, too. Use it for instant napkin rings, tying kids' artwork to chairs, or writing names on wider ribbons for place cards. I tend to burrow

away ribbons from gifts that we've received so there's always some around. This drives my husband crazy, but they're a fun challenge for the kids, who try to find a use for them at the table.

FLOWERS, FRUITS, AND VEGETABLES

I've lived near a spectacular wholesale flower district and I've lived in the rural suburbs where in the winter, flowers could only be found at the local supermarket. Even the ugliest supermarket bouquet can work if you take it apart. Place single flowers, cut short, in a line of water glasses down the center of the table, or weave them around a kitchen island buffet. Think outside of the typical arrangement. Kids seem to be brilliant at this. They have no preconceived notions, so they just create the most playful and beautiful ways to arrange the flowers—for example, all one color, tied in bunches, and floating in teacups. Or they make a collection of leaves and branches from outside in the winter— just check for bugs first.

Incorporate fruits and vegetables into your arrangements. What started as a trend in Paris makes perfect sense at home. Add a few artichokes to a cake stand or platter and fill in with flowers and herbs, for example. Most kids can't pass up a skewer, and are happy to glue a place card onto a toothpick and plunge it into an apple or orange for a friend. Last Thanksgiving when we were snowbound, we laid an extra stalk of Brussels sprouts on its side and surrounded it with votives. Sort of wacky, but it worked. It was as if Jack and his Beanstalk dropped by.

CHAPTER 3 | **A NOTE ON INGREDIENTS**

You probably already own a few cookbooks by big-name chefs. The food they make is exciting to think about, but do those complex recipes really reflect the way you live now? Do you still have a day to make pasta from scratch or drive all over town looking for exotic ingredients such as *bottarga* (dried, salted fish roe) to toss into that pasta? Chances are you don't. But just because ballet class pickup trumps your trip to that great grocery in Chinatown doesn't mean you want to make and serve dumbed-down food. These recipes reflect my curiosity about other cultures and countries—those that I've lived in like Spain, others that I've visited repeatedly, like Greece, and still others that I dream of traveling in, like India. When I'm interested in a country that I've never seen, I visit it by taking a trip to an ethnic market or talking to restaurant owners and talented home cooks for advice.

The ingredients required for my recipes are available no matter where you are. I've lived, shopped, and cooked next to New York City's best gourmet and specialty markets, within steps of the mesmerizing farmers' market in Santa Monica, and also near some questionable supermarkets in rural suburbia. And while we're finally happily settled in the Italian neighborhood of Carroll Gardens in Brooklyn, I shopped for these recipes at fairly typical supermarkets. You won't need to make three trips to five shops to put together a menu from the recipes in this book. Yes, buying organic, farm-raised beef or a nearly extinct, rare breed of heritage pork is ideal when you have the access and income, but the recipes hold their own when made with a supermarket pork loin or roast.

I do think your time and money are well spent supporting local markets and seeking out artisan products like Cowgirl Creamery cheeses and June Taylor jams. There's a list of Playdate Pantry foods on page 170 for your convenience. I've unearthed these items through years of research, my work producing food shows, and sheer luck. Most products are readily available, but there are exceptions. What can I say? I can't live without Spanish smoked paprika or Indian black mustard seeds. Some things are worth the extra time it takes to order from Internet sources, which are provided as well.

○ SPICE TREASURE PLAYDATE ○

I have an obsession with spices. When I was a teenager, anything that seemed exotic made me feel grown up. I constantly reread *Paula Wolfert's Couscous and Other Good Food From Morocco* in bed late at night, and dreamed of spice markets and intricate concoctions. Nowadays, back in the real mom world, spices work their magic by quickly adding a bit of intrigue to basic meats and fish. We also trace the spice routes as a geography lesson at dinner. It's a nice way to point out that "spices" needn't mean "spicy."

I have devised a few activities that help kids find at least one new spice that they like. For example, using cumin seeds with the Tomato Coconut Salsa (page 107), and showing how the hot pepper or chili powder adds the heat.

For these projects, try to buy spices in bulk, at stores like Costco, BJ's, or an ethnic shop where you can buy restaurant-size containers. Otherwise it can get a bit pricey.

Everyone can also make a custom spice blend or dry rub to take home. You can provide a recipe, or they can experiment with their own blend. Layer the spices in small jars that you've provided. I buy small plastic boxes or containers at a party store and supply toothpicks so everyone can create patterns, like sand art. Use stickers and markers to label the containers.

Younger kids can make spice paintings by "painting" pictures or designs with glue and sprinkling the glue with ground spices and mustard seeds, cloves, and colored peppercorns. Just avoid cayenne, and make sure they know not to rub their eyes with spice-covered hands.

MENU

- CURRIED ROASTED CAULIFLOWER (PAGE 103)
- CHINATOWN ROAST PORK (PAGE 71)
- SWEET POTATO SALAD WITH LIME AND ANCHO (PAGE 96)
- SPICY SLAW (PAGE 97)
- PANNA COTTA WITH ROASTED BALSAMIC STRAWBERRIES AND PEPPER (PAGE 144)

Mix spices into softened butter or gently warmed oil to toss with steamed vegetables or sprinkle over roasted meat or fish.

Mix spices into yogurt for crudités or for dipping.

Make a rub for ribs.

CHAPTER 4 | **STARTERS**

A delicious starter is the best way to begin any playdate. It sets the tone, keeps people happily distracted while the rest of the cooking is being finished, and regulates the blood sugar of child and grown-up alike. Choose one great dish, or set up a spread of things that are cheesy, salty, crunchy, and veggie.

The vibe should be a bit of fun and whimsy, with colorful dishes or napkins, pretty Japanese toothpicks or amusing skewers, and glasses that are charming, but not too precious. The point is to make everyone feel relaxed and comfortable. If it's a new group, I always throw in some odd condiment like a slice of Spanish quince paste or exotic cheese to start conversations. Leave a few things for the kids to do, like roll the stuffed dates in nuts or skewer some vegetables into an edible sculpture.

Sometimes you may find yourself wondering, why even sit down to a meal at all? The small-plate restaurant craze works well at home, especially if you're using paper plates. Serve a bunch of the starters and salads and buy a baked ham or a variety of smoked meats and sausages and just graze all day. It's a lazy way to spend a Sunday with friends.

NO-FRY CANDIED SPICED PECANS

This recipe was a breakthrough for me. Every year, I used to fry batches of nuts for the holidays. But the mess and smell of oil, not to mention the safety concerns connected with using quantities of 350-degree oil while excited kids were running in and out of the kitchen, had taken me pretty far away from the holiday joy I was going for. After much tinkering, I re-created the caramel crunch and glossy sheen that I got from frying, by roasting the sweet-and-spicy nut mixture. Now I make these *with* the kids, instead of fearing for their safety. They especially love tossing the nuts into the goop.

2 egg whites

1 tablespoon kosher salt

1 tablespoon freshly ground pepper

2 teaspoons Hungarian sweet paprika

1 cup confectioners' sugar

½ cup corn syrup

1 pound whole pecans, shelled

○ Preheat the oven to 375 degrees F. Prepare a baking sheet with a silicone mat or cover it with foil and grease lightly with a neutral oil like vegetable or canola.

○ In a medium bowl, beat the egg whites until frothy. Mix in the remaining ingredients, except the nuts, stirring until well combined. Add the nuts and toss to coat well.

○ Spread out evenly on the baking sheet and bake for 20 minutes, stirring occasionally. The nuts will stick together a bit. Let them cool slightly and then carefully separate any clumps. Allow to cool completely before packing in a metal container or wrapping tightly in foil. (A plastic container will make the nuts soggy.) The nuts will keep for about 10 days.

SERVES 4 TO 6

NOTE For spicier nuts, add a few pinches of cayenne.

○ **KIDS IN THE KITCHEN** ○

Older kids can crack and separate the eggs, and measure and mix the ingredients (make sure hands are washed immediately, as spices can sting the eyes). Younger kids can stir, help spread the nuts on the baking sheet, and pack them when cool.

MOZZARELLA WITH LEMON, BAY LEAVES, AND CAPERS

My kids are nuts about anything shaped like a ball, so it was no surprise when Mathias grabbed a big container of *bocconcini*—little mozzarella balls—at Costco. They look like such fun, can you really blame him? This marinade has a bright lemony flavor with a bit of bitterness from the bay leaf and saltiness from the capers, which I really like instead of the hot red pepper flakes usually sprinkled over *bocconcini*.

Make this a day or at least 4 hours in advance for the best flavor. It will keep in the refrigerator for a few days. It's easily multiplied for large parties; just make sure you bring it to room temperature before serving. Finishing the dish with a sprinkle of coarse sea salt adds a bit of crunch and perks up the flavor.

One 1-pound container mozzarella balls
(bocconcini), drained

½ teaspoon kosher salt

1 lemon, washed

1 cup extra-virgin olive oil

4 dried bay leaves

8 black peppercorns

3 cloves garlic, peeled

1 tablespoon capers, rinsed

Coarse sea salt and freshly ground pepper
to taste

Crusty bread, toasted pita bread, or crackers
for serving

- Carefully pat the cheese dry and place in a large bowl. Sprinkle the salt evenly over the cheese and gently rub into the cheese. Taste first; you can omit the salt if the cheese is unusually salty. Set aside.

- Using a vegetable peeler, peel the zest from the lemon in large strips, taking care not to take off too much of the bitter white pith. Juice the lemon and reserve 3 tablespoons of the juice; discard the rest or save for other use.

- Combine the oil, lemon zest, bay leaves, peppercorns, and garlic in a small saucepan over low heat and bring to a gentle simmer. Turn off the heat and set the oil aside to cool to room temperature. Remove the peppercorns from the oil and add the reserved lemon juice and the capers. Pour the oil over the cheese and toss gently.

- When ready to serve, sprinkle with coarse sea salt and serve alongside crusty bread, toasted pita, or crackers. Or serve as individual bruschetta; drizzle the flavored oil on top of toasted bread, top with cheese and capers, and sprinkle with coarse sea salt and freshly ground pepper.

SERVES 4 TO 6

◦ KIDS IN THE KITCHEN ◦

Kids of any age can help measure ingredients, salt the cheese, squeeze the lemon, rinse the capers, and taste for seasoning. Older kids can peel off the lemon zest, remove the peppercorns from the cooked oil, toss the cheese, and help with presentation.

STUFFED DATES

I tend to avoid fussy hors d'oeuvres, but I can't deny there is something inherently glamorous about bite-sized, delicious treats. The kids can do all the work on these. Just make sure the younger ones get spoons to remove the pits if they aren't old enough to use knives. Try local or artisanal cheeses, like Maytag Blue, a flavored goat cheese, or my favorite, Humboldt Fog, a mild goat cheese marked with a thin layer of ash, from Cypress Hill in northern California.

½ pound blue or goat cheese

18 dates, halved and pitted

½ cup salted pistachios, shelled and coarsely chopped

½ cup pine nuts, toasted (see Note)

○ Press a small amount of cheese into each date. Roll half of the cheese-filled dates into the pistachios and the other half into the pine nuts. Arrange on a platter and serve.

SERVES 8 TO 10

VARIATIONS Replace the nuts with smoked paprika, seasoned salt, coarsely ground pepper, or chopped fresh herbs to vary the flavor and presentation.

NOTE To toast the nuts, sauté them in a dry pan over medium-low heat, stirring frequently, until they are light golden brown and fragrant, about 1 minute. Or toast them in a 325 degree F oven for about 3 minutes, shaking the pan midway through baking.

○ **KIDS IN THE KITCHEN** ○

Kids of all ages can pit the dates, stuff with cheese, roll in nuts, and place on trays for serving.

MEET THE NEIGHBORS / MEDITERRANEAN MIXER

The best part of living in Los Angeles was embracing the chaos and messiness of real entertaining—tripping over the kids while racing to the grill, a friend (or better yet, a wine-maker) bringing the wine, effortlessly picked up in the supermarket. Anthony's news of a job-related move back East to a new neighborhood in New York meant a major change, but I became militant about not losing the best parts of California living. Being in the insane nesting phase and desperate for friendly neighbors (I was eight months pregnant and Mathias was eighteen months old) I went into overdrive and planned this ode to California with an open house. It worked because I made sure most things could be served at room temperature. I bought a bunch of dried sausages, let Mathias mash the cheese in the dates, and roasted new potatoes to fill in the rest of the menu. You can also just buy cookies or dessert.

MENU

- ZUCCHINI AND MINT BRUSCHETTA (served like a dip with store-bought crackers) (PAGE 45)

- DRIED SAUSAGES AND CHEESES, QUINCE PASTE, GRAPES, ETC.

- STUFFED DATES (PAGE 36)

- SLOW-COOKED SALMON WITH SALSA VERDE (served at room temperature) (PAGE 65)

- BALSAMIC CHERRY TOMATO SALAD (PAGE 104)

- ROASTED NEW POTATOES

- HONEY AND LIME FRUIT SALAD (PAGE 121)

- LEMON POLENTA CAKE (PAGE 117)

1-2-3 CHEESE TART

Roll, stir, and bake—those steps are the "one, two, three" of this recipe's title, and it really is that easy to make. Tangy cheese in a buttery crust is a welcome change of pace from the expected cheese plate. And since most children can whip this up on their own, the recipe is an instant winner. Most of the ingredients are easy to keep around, so you can make this tart at a moment's notice. By all means play with different cheeses, just make sure to use the ricotta for the creaminess. Instead of the feta, try Cheddar, blue, or even something like *kashkaval* from the Balkans, if you can find it. This irresistible tart is a natural for cocktails or a light supper with a salad.

1 sheet best-quality frozen puff pastry, such as Pepperidge Farm or Dufour

1 cup ricotta cheese

½ cup grated aged provolone or Parmesan cheese

½ cup crumbled feta cheese

1 egg

¼ teaspoon kosher salt

½ teaspoon freshly ground pepper

Chopped fresh thyme, oregano, or rosemary for garnish

- Preheat the oven to 400 degrees F.

- On a lightly floured surface, roll out the pastry into a thin rectangle, 11 by 13 inches and about ¼ inch thick. Transfer to a baking sheet or rimmed half sheet pan. Prick the dough all over with a fork to prevent the tart base from bubbling up.

- In a medium bowl, mix the cheeses, egg, salt, and pepper. Spread over the dough, leaving a ½-inch border. Brush the edges lightly with water, fold over the sides of the dough, and press them to create an edge, pinching the corners and pulling them to make small points like the tip of a star. (The tart can be refrigerated for up to 8 hours before baking. However, you may need to slightly increase the baking time.)

- Bake for 25 to 30 minutes, until the cheese is golden and bubbly, and the sides and bottom of the crust are dark golden brown, making sure that they don't burn. Let the tart rest for a minute, then cut into 2-inch squares, sprinkle with fresh herbs, and serve.

SERVES 6 TO 8

NOTES Defrost the pastry overnight in the fridge, or for a half-hour or so on the counter. The pastry should be able to be rolled easily when ready; if not, allow it to sit until it is pliable, but not too warm.

If you are using the Parmesan and a mild feta, you may want to add an additional ¼ teaspoon or so of kosher salt. Or taste a square after baking and if it needs salt, simply sprinkle salt over the top of the tart.

⊙ KIDS IN THE KITCHEN ⊙

Older kids can make this with little supervision. Younger kids may need help, but they can roll the puff pastry, crack the egg, mix the cheeses and egg, brush the dough with water, form the tart, and scatter the herbs.

GRAZE ALL DAY

When it comes to dinner parties, we're all so used to thinking in terms of the main course. But the tyranny of the main dish need not hold you hostage any longer. You can put together a combination of starters and snacks to make a meal. The small-plate dining trend is a great way to entertain at home when you set out a mixture of things you've made and things you've bought or have in the pantry. Crudités can be casually arranged on a large platter or a few different plates or glasses. I amuse the kids with a few offbeat vegetables like red carrots, broccolini, or purple string beans. Serve them with a Sour Cream and Scallion Dip (page 44), hummus topped with orange oil and smoked paprika, or anything creamy, and kids are more apt to eat veggies. If they're old enough add a handful of skewers. They'll eat just about anything if it's on the end of a spear, even if it's broccoli.

Arrange artisanal olive, fennel raisin, or locally baked breads or some crackers with an assortment of sliced salamis and hams. Assemble a cheese platter. My general rule is buy local and try something new. Then balance the offering with a selection of hard cheeses (such as Cheddar, Gruyére, or Manchego), soft ones (a log of goat rolled in salt, pepper, and herbs, or a slice of Boucheron), mild (locally made mozzarella or Havarti or Muenster), runny (Taleggio or Camembert), and stinky or tangy (Maytag Blue or Époisse). Find a good cheese market, don't be afraid to ask for tastes, and when in doubt, grab a fine Cheddar like Keen's from England, or anything from northern California's Cowgirl Creamery, especially their creamy Red Hawk or Mount Tam; see Sources, page 173. Add a fancy restaurant cheese course flourish and introduce some sweet or sour notes to fill out the platter. Cheese shops and departments offer an array of items, as easy or exotic as you're up for—a small dish of honey, a chunk of honeycomb, a slice of quince paste or dried figs, or an imported spoon fruit like Italian *mostarda* (a rich cooked fruit jam with the tang of mustard and vinegar) or cherry jam.

Small fruits like lady apples, Seckel pears, clementines, and apricots look gorgeous in a shallow bowl or platter, and are the perfect size for the younger set. Tuck in tiny bites of Lauren's Lemon Squares (page 125), and offer the giant Polka-Dot Linzertorte (page 119) as well. Or have the kids make some Chocolate Candy Crunch (page 146) to serve with store-bought ice cream.

I usually set everything out on the kitchen island—or a table far from the kitchen if I'm feeling frazzled. For the kids, try fancy juices from Ceres or Looza to mix with water or seltzer, while the adults can have a fun cocktail or a glass of whichever wine we're currently obsessed with. I no longer have enough of any matched plates or glasses for a very big gathering, but by keeping everything in the same color range or just using white with colored paper or washable linens and some casual flowers, the overall look of the party is coherent, fun, and a little bit funky.

GRAZE ALL DAY MENU

- MOZZARELLA WITH LEMON, BAY LEAVES, AND CAPERS (PAGE 35)
- BREADS, CRACKERS, CRUDITÉS, OR PARMESAN FINGERS (PAGE 83)
- SOUR CREAM AND SCALLION DIP (PAGE 44) OR EDAMAME DIP (PAGE 41)
- PICKLED SHRIMP WITH MANGO AND FENNEL (PAGE 47)
- STORE-BOUGHT HAM/SMOKED TURKEY
- SNOW WHITE'S SALAD (PAGE 105)
- LAUREN'S LEMON SQUARES (PAGE 125)
- POLKA-DOT LINZERTORTE (PAGE 119)
- CHOCOLATE CANDY CRUNCH (PAGE 146)

EDAMAME DIP

I'm crazy about the salty fresh soybeans you can order in sushi bars—*edamame* in Japanese. They're the ones you crack out of their fuzzy green shells and simply can't stop eating. I was really excited when I found them frozen in my local health food store, but I later realized they were already shelled. They weren't as much fun to eat, so I decided to whiz them around in the food processor for a fresh take on the usual white bean or hummus spread. Mathias and Natasha get a kick out of the bright green color, and the slightly chunky texture works well when served with thin rice crackers. Now I'm never without a few bags in the freezer for this dip or to toss into leftover fried rice or a salad.

One 1-pound bag frozen shelled edamame (soybeans)

1 tablespoon toasted sesame oil

2 tablespoons neutral oil, such as canola or vegetable

1 tablespoon seasoned rice vinegar

1 teaspoon kosher salt

½ teaspoon freshly ground pepper

Juice of 1 lime

Rice crackers or crudités such as baby carrots, sliced fennel, radishes, blanched broccoli, or string beans, for serving

Combine the ingredients in the bowl of a food processor, and run on low until smooth. You can add a teaspoon or so of water if it seems too thick to spread. Serve with rice crackers or crudités.

SERVES 6 TO 8

◦ KIDS IN THE KITCHEN ◦

Kids of all ages (supervise the younger ones) can measure the ingredients, wash vegetables for crudités, push the pulse button on the food processor, spoon the dip in the bowl, and arrange the crackers and crudités. Older kids might like to practice their knife skills by cutting the vegetables into different shapes.

SEARED WRAPPED SCALLOPS WITH BALSAMIC GLAZE

Bobby Flay is one of the most committed dads I know (after my husband, Anthony, of course!) When I was producing his show at Lifetime, he was constantly on my case to stop working so hard so I could start working on having kids. He was right, of course. One of the other things we share, besides parental pride, is a love of all things Spanish. I lived in Spain for a year after college, and shortly after I returned, Bobby opened his Spanish-influenced restaurant, Bolo. This was way before the public's current love affair with Iberian food began. He's been a great cheerleader for my career, and when I told him about *Kitchen Playdates,* he generously provided this recipe. Bobby's succulent dish included fig vinegar, which isn't easy to find. I substituted brown sugar and balsamic and changed the presentation so that kids can wrap the scallops with the ham.

⅓ cup balsamic vinegar, plus more to taste

½ teaspoon dark brown sugar

12 large sea scallops, little "foot" removed

Kosher salt and freshly ground pepper

½ pound Serrano ham or prosciutto, thinly sliced

1 tablespoon extra-virgin olive oil

Fresh rosemary or thyme, finely chopped, for garnish

◉ Combine the vinegar and sugar in a small saucepan and boil over high heat to reduce until syrupy, about 3 to 4 minutes, stirring occasionally. Set aside.

◉ Season the scallops with salt and pepper. Wrap a slice of ham around the wide, flat top and bottom of each scallop. If needed, place a toothpick horizontally through the scallop to secure the ham.

◉ Heat a large sauté pan over medium-high heat, add the olive oil, and heat until shimmering. Carefully place scallops, ham side down, in the pan. Cook until the ham is crisp, about 1 to 2 minutes. Carefully turn the scallops and continue to cook for another 1 to 2 minutes.

◉ Remove the toothpicks and transfer 3 scallops to each plate, leaning each slightly towards the center like a tepee for presentation. Drizzle with the balsamic mixture. Sprinkle with freshly ground pepper and the chopped herbs.

SERVES 4

NOTE To make a full tray to set out for a buffet, wrap the scallops ahead, and roast them on an oiled baking sheet for 10 minutes at 400 degrees F. Arrange them on a tray or platter, drizzle with the balsamic syrup, spear with toothpicks, and serve.

◦ KIDS IN THE KITCHEN ◦

Kids of all ages can season and wrap the scallops, spear them with toothpicks (with some adult supervision), and garnish them with fresh herbs.

SOUR CREAM AND SCALLION DIP

While trying to make a caramelized onion dip for the Burger Bar the night before a birthday party (see page 68), I got distracted and ended up overcooking the onions until they were bitter, blackened, and totally unusable. Fortunately, I had some scallions left over from the Sweet Potato Salad (page 96), and I quickly sautéed them with a jalapeño and some chopped garlic. It was a hit. This variation is faster, since the scallions need less attention than the onions. It adds more contrast when served with sweet potato chips. The dip is even better when made the day before so the flavors mingle a bit.

4 bunches scallions, thinly sliced

2 tablespoons olive oil

1 jalapeño, seeded, deribbed, and finely chopped

2 cloves garlic, finely chopped

1½ cups sour cream

Zest and juice of 2 limes

1 teaspoon kosher salt

½ teaspoon freshly ground pepper

Sweet potato or blue corn chips for serving

○ Set aside about a quarter of the sliced scallions for a garnish. In a large sauté pan, heat the oil over medium heat and add the remaining scallions and the jalapeño. Cook until the vegetables have softened and the scallions are pale gold, about 5 minutes. Add the garlic and sauté for 1 minute. Remove from the heat and let cool slightly.

○ Put the sour cream in a medium bowl. Add the lime zest and juice, the salt, pepper, and the scallion mixture and stir. Garnish with the reserved scallions, and serve with chips.

SERVES 4 TO 6

○ **KIDS IN THE KITCHEN** ○

Older kids can practice their knife skills by slicing the scallions, and they can zest the limes. The younger ones can help measure the ingredients, juice the limes, mix the dip, and serve.

ZUCCHINI AND MINT BRUSCHETTA

On a beautiful summer evening, I like to steal away into the backyard with a cold glass of rosé and the excuse that I need peace and quiet to concentrate on slowly grilling the zucchini for these bruschetta over a low fire. Anthony or my mom happily babysits. They know it won't be long before I return to coarsely chop the zucchini so the kids can mix it with lemon, mint, and a touch of garlic. Then they can slather the mixture over toasted bread. You can make this a day in advance since the dip keeps well in the refrigerator overnight. Or have a teen do the grilling and relax in the hammock.

⅓ cup olive oil

Zest and juice of 1 lemon

½ teaspoon kosher salt

Freshly ground pepper to taste

4 medium zucchini, ends trimmed, sliced lengthwise ¼ inch thick

¼ cup finely chopped fresh mint

2 cloves garlic, finely chopped

1 loaf Italian or country bread, or a baguette, thinly sliced

- Prepare a low to medium grill.

- In a roasting pan or 9-by-11-inch baking dish, mix the oil, lemon zest and juice, salt, and pepper. Put the zucchini (in batches, if necessary) in the oil mixture and let sit for about 2 minutes. Remove the zucchini, allowing the excess oil to drain back into the pan, and place the zucchini on the grill. Reserve the oil mixture.

- Grill the zucchini for 5 to 8 minutes, turning occasionally. They should be golden brown in spots and soft, rather than firm.

- Allow the zucchini to cool slightly, coarsely chop, and place in a bowl. Add the mint, chopped garlic, and a bit of the oil and lemon mixture to taste. Season again with salt and pepper.

- Prepare the toasts: Lightly oil both sides of each slice of bread and grill until golden brown, or toast in the oven.

SERVES 4 TO 6

NOTE In the winter, grill the zucchini and the toasts in a cast-iron grill pan over medium heat. The cooking time may be slightly longer.

◦ KIDS IN THE KITCHEN ◦

Older kids can slice the zucchini while supervised. Halve the zucchini to make it easier for them. They can also chop the grilled zucchini; allow it to cool slightly for safer handling. Younger kids can measure ingredients, mix the marinade, and oil the bread. If you'd like, let the kids top the toasts and pass them around, or have them spoon the dip into a bowl and serve with stacks of the toasts.

PICKLED SHRIMP WITH MANGO AND FENNEL

There's something about mango and shrimp that is just so good, so cheerful, and, well, so *right*. Pickling the shrimp, and adding fennel slivers give this dish a fresh take on shrimp with mango salsa. If you like, buy precooked shrimp and throw it all together the night before to let the flavors get acquainted. You can easily multiply this recipe. It looks gorgeous in a big trifle bowl or individual martini glasses if you are making a single batch.

1 red onion, thinly sliced

1 fennel bulb, halved and thinly sliced (trimmings saved)

2 lemons, washed and very thinly sliced

1 tablespoon salt

1 pound large shrimp (13 to 15 per pound), peeled and deveined, with tails left on

1 mango, sliced into thin half-moons

1 cup extra virgin olive oil

½ cup fresh lemon juice

¼ cup rice wine vinegar

6 cloves garlic, peeled and crushed

1 teaspoon fennel seeds

1 tablespoon black peppercorns

1 tablespoon coriander seeds, lightly cracked (see Note)

½ teaspoon kosher or sea salt

○ Combine the onion, fennel trimmings, and half the sliced lemons in a large pot filled with cold water. Bring to a boil, lower the heat, and simmer for 15 minutes. Add the salt and shrimp. Remove from the heat and allow the shrimp to cook until they just turn pink and begin to curl, about 45 seconds to 1 minute. Drain, and let shrimp cool.

○ Combine all the remaining ingredients in a large bowl, add the shrimp, cover, and refrigerate overnight. Toss with the kosher or sea salt before serving.

SERVES 4 TO 6

NOTE To crack the coriander seeds, place in a plastic bag and roll or whack lightly with a rolling pin or the back of a pan.

○ **KIDS IN THE KITCHEN** ○

Younger ones can help measure the ingredients, crack coriander seeds, and serve. Older kids can peel and devein the shrimp under supervision. Cookware shops sell shrimp deveiners that kids can use instead of more dangerous paring knives.

GRANDMA BEA'S CHOPPED STRING BEANS

One of the best parties we have ever had—pre-kids—was the "Come Dressed as Your Favorite Tacky Hors d'Oeuvre Party." Our guests didn't dress exactly as an hors d'oeuvre, but in the spirit. There were lots of saris and matador capes, for example. Our friend Nancy Herrmann took the subway with her greasy hair, a housedress, and flip-flops while carrying mystery meat roll-ups in little plastic bags, and won a fifty-pack of pigs in the blanket from Costco. My food world friends said it was some of the best food and laughs they'd had in years. The Russian-born food writer Anya von Bremzen brought "herring in a fur coat," a layered beet, herring, and sour cream dish. My entry was a sentimental favorite, my grandmother's version of mock chopped liver, an oniony dip that's perfect for rye crackers. I'm warning you: It's ugly as sin, but sinfully good.

¼ cup vegetable oil

2 onions, thinly sliced

4 ½ cups string beans, trimmed

3 cups peeled chunks of carrot

2 hard-boiled eggs

2 teaspoons kosher salt

¼ teaspoon freshly ground pepper

2 to 3 tablespoons mayonnaise

1 teaspoon chopped fresh dill, plus some extra sprigs for garnish

Caraway rye crackers or rye melba toast for serving

○ Heat the oil in a large sauté pan over medium-high heat. Add the onions and sauté, stirring frequently, until dark golden brown. Meanwhile, in a large saucepan fitted with a metal steamer, steam the string beans and carrots together until very tender, about 8 to 10 minutes. The string beans should be past the bright and crunchy stage and look more like cafeteria food. The carrots should be very soft.

○ In the bowl of a food processor, combine the onions, beans, carrots, eggs, salt, and pepper. Pulse until a coarse mixture is formed. Transfer to a serving bowl and stir in the mayonnaise and chopped dill. Taste for salt and pepper, and garnish with dill sprigs. Serve with crackers.

SERVES 4 TO 6

○ KIDS IN THE KITCHEN ○

Younger kids can trim the beans by snapping them off with their fingers; older ones can use knives under supervision. Most kids can peel hard-boiled eggs, measure ingredients, stir, and serve the mixture with crackers.

GRANDMA BEA'S BEEF AND BARLEY SOUP

This is my one true comfort food, the soup that always tasted as if my grandmother made it *just* for me. Eighteen years ago I asked her to send me the recipe from Florida so I could share the love with Anthony. Imagine my surprise when I read the first ingredient: "1 package of Vegetable Soup Mix with Mushrooms from Manischewitz." It was not exactly the treasured family secret I expected. But when I made the soup myself, it tasted just like Beatie's. So seek out the kosher aisle of your local supermarket and dig around in the cardboard bins for a few cellophane tubes of the soup mix. (Make sure you grab the veggie one; they make a few.) You won't be disappointed; it's a shortcut you won't taste in the soup bowl. And like many things your grandmother made, it's even better the next day.

One 6-ounce package Manischewitz Vegetable Soup Mix with Mushrooms

5 beef flanken bones (about 1½ pounds; see Notes)

7 cups water

4 carrots, peeled and cut into ½-inch rounds

3 celery stalks, thinly sliced

1 small onion, diced

2 teaspoons kosher salt, plus more to taste

3 tablespoons chopped fresh dill

Freshly ground pepper

Buttered rye bread for serving

◎ Remove the soup base packet from the tube and reserve. In a large stockpot over high heat, combine the remaining ingredients in the tube, the bones, and water. As the mixture comes to a boil, lower the heat, because as Bea warns, "It will *run* over your stove." (And because boiling the bones will result in a fatty stock.) Lower the heat and skim the foam from the soup.

◎ Add the carrots, celery, onion, and the reserved soup base packet. Add the salt and simmer the soup for 2 hours, skimming the foam as needed. Add the dill and salt and pepper to taste. Serve with the buttered rye bread.

SERVES 4

NOTES Flanken bones are simply short ribs that have been cut lengthwise rather than between the bones. The meat is very tender and the bones add a depth of flavor to the soup. You can substitute an equal weight of short ribs if your market doesn't carry them.

I like this soup to be thick. If it seems a bit thin, add a handful of rice or orzo toward the end and simmer until cooked.

The soup freezes well; make a double batch, allow to cool, and freeze half in an airtight container for up to 2 months.

◎ **KIDS IN THE KITCHEN** ◎

Older kids can chop the vegetables and help skim the soup. Younger ones can wash the dill and butter the rye bread for serving.

PIZZA PARTY PLAYDATE

At this pizza party, kids get to spin pies, spin tunes, and even spin art. Set aside a pound of dough, or a pie's worth per child. While it may seem excessive, they can play with it for hours. Whether you buy it at the local parlor or in the freezer section of your supermarket, premade pizza dough is a busy parent's best friend. You can use it to make almost anything: traditional pizza, grilled pizza, and stuffed breads, to be sure; but also pretzels and even yummy chocolate calzones. Try any of these variations for a sticky, fun mess that keeps everyone busy, happy, and well fed. You'll wonder how you ever survived without frozen dough.

Set up a separate table with a spin art machine to keep the kids busy while everything is baking, and set out salamis, olives, cheeses, grilled sausages and vegetables, and a big salad to stave off hunger while they play and the pizzas bake.

ROLLING OUT THE DOUGH AND BAKING IT

One pound of dough makes 1 large pie or can be divided to make 4 individual pies. If the dough has been frozen, defrost it overnight in the fridge, or take it out first thing on the day you are planning to serve. Have an extra pound hidden away for insurance.

On a lightly floured work surface press the dough into a thin circle. (Thin pizzas will cook more evenly.) Don't get hung up on perfect circles, whatever shape the kids (or you) wind up with is fine—I call it a continent or map so no one's feelings are hurt.

If you like a crunchy crust, you can add a handful of cornmeal to the white flour on the work surface and roll the dough over that mixture.

Position one oven rack in the middle and the other on the bottom third, and then preheat the oven to 450 degrees F. If you have a pizza stone, slide the pie with its toppings onto the stone. If not, cook the pizza on an oiled sheet pan. Then remove it halfway through the cooking time and slide the pie directly onto the oven rack. Continue to cook until the top is bubbling and the bottom crust is golden brown, about 10 to 12 minutes total.

Or if the weather's right, grill the pizzas. Prepare a grill so that it is hot on one side and low on the other. Brush both sides of the dough lightly with oil. Place on the hot side of the grill and cook until the bottom has a firm crust with grill marks. Slide the dough over to the cooler side of the grill and add the toppings. You will have to slide the dough back and forth over the heat for a few minutes until the top is bubbling and any cheese has melted, about 5 to 7 minutes.

ARTICHOKE PIZZA

For a slightly more sophisticated take on your basic red sauce pizza, defrost one 9-ounce package of frozen artichoke hearts, dry them well, and toss with ¼ cup of olive oil, ½ teaspoon of salt, ¼ teaspoon of freshly ground pepper, 1 teaspoon of lemon juice, and 1 tablespoon of chopped fresh thyme or rosemary. Top the pizza dough with the artichokes and bake at 450 degrees F for 15 to 20 minutes. Midway through baking, crumble ¼ pound of goat cheese on top along with ¼ cup of grated Parmesan cheese.

STUFFED PIZZA SNAKES

When my kids make calzones, I find that they eat the bread and ignore the filling, after I've spent all that time and energy hiding healthful things inside. With a long snake of stuffed pizza, they tend to eat the whole enchilada, so to speak. Adults can put them away, too. I went to a New Year's Eve party last year where Gregory Demiris, who runs the lake concession at Woodbridge Lake in Goshen, Connecticut, held a crowd of well-dressed sophisticates enthralled with his sausage and spinach roll. We ate the roll, adapted here, with the best Champagne, and it turned out to be a very good year.

Remove ¼ pound of sweet Italian fennel sausage links from their casings and sauté over medium-high heat until no longer pink. Add a 10-ounce package of defrosted and drained frozen spinach (or fresh if you prefer) and 2 cloves of garlic, peeled and slightly smashed, and sauté. Season with salt and pepper. Allow the filling to cool slightly and discard the garlic.

Roll a 1-pound piece of pizza dough into a rectangle about 5 inches wide by 17 inches long. Transfer to an oiled baking sheet. Spread the filling down the center. Sprinkle the filling with ¼ cup of grated pecorino cheese and ½ pound of grated mozzarella cheese. Bring the sides of the dough together, and press them closed. Press the ends closed. Roll until the seam side is down. Twist into an "S" shape, like a snake. Brush with oil and sprinkle with sesame seeds or kosher salt.

Bake at 450 degrees F for 20 to 25 minutes, or until the dough is cooked through. (Insert the point of a knife to make certain.)

CHOCOLATE PIZZA STICKS

Can you tell this is a snowstorm creation? Knead 1 cup of chocolate chips into 1 pound of pizza dough. Let the dough rest for about 30 minutes. Cut into 8 pieces and form into pretzel shapes, twisted sticks, or any other shape that inspires you, and place on a lightly oiled sheet. Brush the dough with vegetable oil, sprinkle with colored sugar, and bake at 450 degrees F for about 15 to 20 minutes, until cooked through.

CHOCOLATE RICOTTA CALZONES

Make Chocolate Pizza Sticks dough and divide into pieces. Mix ½ pound of ricotta cheese with 1 egg, 1 ½ tablespoons of sugar, and ½ teaspoon of cinnamon. Roll or press each piece of dough into a 5- to 6-inch circle. Place a few spoonfuls of filling in the center of each circle, fold over the dough to make a half-moon, and crimp closed. Brush with vegetable oil and sprinkle with sugar. Bake at 450 degrees F for 25 minutes.

STOCKING UP FOR FANCY COCKTAILS AND MOCKTAILS

I always used to be early for dinner reservations, and would wait at the bar for my dinner companion, sampling the latest cocktail. Well, all that waiting actually paid off because I learned a thing or two from the bartenders. And now that I'm a perpetually late mom, I highly recommend a distracting signature drink to hand off to prompt guests while you hunt for your lipstick. If your pantry is well stocked and the fridge has the best-quality juices and some simple syrup (see below) you can pull off a special cocktail or mocktail without any advance notice. It's always a good idea to get in a few practice sessions with your spouse or a couple of friends, though.

CERES, LOOZA, OR SIMILAR BRANDS OF FANCY JUICES Guava, passion fruit, apricot, and peach make a refreshing change from the standard OJ and grapefruit. These juices mix well with seltzer, rum, or just about anything. Splash some juice into the blender with yogurt and bananas for a smoothie (page 167).

LITCHIS IN SYRUP These are usually found at an Asian grocer, or in the ethnic food aisle. The perfumed fruits are canned with a sugary syrup. Stir a few drops of the syrup into vodka (or club soda for the younger set) and garnish with litchis for a litchi martini.

COLORED SUGARS These are the same sugars that you would use for decorating baked goods. When you trace the rim of a glass with a lemon or lime wedge and dip into colored sugar the glass screams instant party. Try it with sturdy drinking glasses for the kids and fill with their favorite juice and club soda combos.

VANILLA VODKA I'm usually not one for a sweet alcohol, but when my Aunt Linda mixed this with a bit of peppermint schnapps and coated the glass rims with crushed candy canes, I became a convert. The kids adore the candy cane rims. Try rimming plastic cups filled with chocolate milk, or mugs of hot chocolate.

POMEGRANATE JUICE Typically found in the refrigerated section, pomegranate juice is usually unsweetened. Use in place of cranberry, but add a bit of sugar or simple syrup (recipe follows).

LEMONADE I prefer the Odwalla brand, but stock your favorite kind, or have the kids squeeze a batch, and blend with strawberries or watermelon, or with a splash of simple syrup, and handfuls of chopped fresh mint.

GINGER ALE We really don't keep soda in the house, but for a treat, we mix ginger ale with a citrus juice and a few cherries in syrup. It's our version of a Shirley Temple.

SIMPLE SYRUP To make simple syrup, simmer 2 parts sugar with 1 part water until the sugar dissolves, about 3 minutes. Allow to cool and store in the fridge for up to a week. A few spoonfuls will sweeten most any cocktail or mocktail.

MOJITOS Add 2 cups of chopped fresh mint and 2/3 cup of freshly squeezed lime juice to 3/4 cup slightly cooled simple syrup. Transfer to an ice cube tray and freeze. When ready to use, place cubes in a blender with one jigger of light rum per cube and blend. Pour into a glass, and add a splash of club soda for a fast mojito. Blend with pineapple juice and a splash of soda for a mocktail.

STUFFED OLIVES Try Santa Barbara brand, or other brand of olive stuffed with jalapeños, anchovies, or lemon peel. Add an olive or two and a splash of the salty liquid into gin or vodka for a dirty martini, or throw a few into the kids' tomato juice.

PARMESAN SHORTBREAD

These savory, cheesy shortbreads are a refreshing change from cheese and crackers, and if you tend to keep a nice hunk of Parmesan in the fridge, you can whip them up any old time. Try a variety of cheeses, too. This is a good way to use up random leftover bits. Sometimes I make the dough on a Wednesday or Thursday night when the kids are watching a movie, and refrigerate it and bake the shortbreads for a Friday night movie date at home with Anthony. I just throw together a salad, put the shortbreads on a plate with some dried sausages and olives, and open a bottle of Brunello. They freeze really well, and I often wrap them in cellophane to give to friends.

1 cup (2 sticks) butter

2 cups all-purpose flour

2½ cups grated Parmesan cheese

½ teaspoon kosher salt

○ Put all the ingredients in the bowl of a food processor and process until the dough just starts to come together, but before it forms a ball. Dump the dough onto a large sheet of plastic, and lift the plastic to gently form the dough into a brick that is 4 by 6 inches, and is about ¾ inch thick. Chill for at least 1 hour or overnight. If you are in a rush, you can also freeze the dough for 20 to 30 minutes.

○ Preheat the oven to 350 degrees F.

○ Line a baking sheet with a silicone mat or lightly butter.

○ Cut the dough crosswise into shortbread fingers about ½ inch thick. Or, for even more fun, have the kids cut it into stars or other shapes with cookie cutters. Bake for 25 to 30 minutes until lightly browned.

SERVES 6 TO 8

VARIATIONS Try adding ¼ teaspoon of chopped fresh rosemary, or replace ⅓ cup of the flour with cornmeal for a bit of crunch.

○ **KIDS IN THE KITCHEN** ○

Kids of all ages can measure the ingredients, form and cut the dough, and stack for serving.

STICKY WINGS

I spent one cold college year in Buffalo and warmed myself with countless versions of the eponymous local wings. But it was a trip to a Singapore food market that redefined the perfect wing for me: sticky, but also a little spicy and sweet—the perfect thing to nibble with a cold beer. Now that we have kids, I tend to let people put on their own hot sauce rather than add it to the marinade, which makes the wings very family friendly.

You can certainly use preground spices. I tend to be a fanatic and grind my own whenever possible. You can't beat the intensity of flavor, and my kids love to run the coffee grinder/spice mill. I think it helps them understand what different spices are, so they don't equate the word "spice" with "hot" and "grown-ups only."

2 tablespoons coriander seeds

1 tablespoon fennel seeds

1 tablespoon cumin seeds

½ cup light brown sugar

⅔ cup molasses

1 cup soy sauce

8 cloves garlic, peeled and smashed

One 4-inch piece ginger, thinly sliced

5½ pounds chicken wings

- In a small sauté pan over medium-high heat, toast the seeds (or ground spices if using) for about 30 seconds, stirring frequently until fragrant and taking care not to burn. Grind the seeds and place in a large bowl. Add all the remaining ingredients except the chicken wings and stir until well combined. To marinate, divide the wings between 2 large plastic zip bags. Divide the marinade between the bags, seal, and place on a baking sheet to catch any spills. Refrigerate overnight, turning the bags a few times to evenly distribute the marinade.

- Preheat the oven to 425 degrees F.

- Remove the wings from the marinade, and reserve the marinade. Place the wings on foil-covered baking sheets. Bake for 35 to 40 minutes, until fully cooked, turning once halfway through the baking time.

- Strain the marinade and bring to a boil over medium-high heat. Cook until the marinade is reduced to a sticky glaze, about 15 to 20 minutes.

- Toss the fully cooked wings in the glaze and serve.

SERVES 6 TO 8

NOTE The wings can be baked and glazed a day ahead of time. Rewarm in a 325 degree F oven for about 10 to 15 minutes.

○ **KIDS IN THE KITCHEN** ○

Most kids can measure the spices and ingredients, and older ones can toast and grind the spices under supervision.

VIDEO COOKBOOK PLAYDATE

Some of my most treasured possessions are the handwritten recipes from my mom and my grandmothers, Sylvia and Bea. Some are on formal index cards. Others are on scraps of paper that tell their own stories. I wish I had been smart enough to videotape my grandmothers cooking, to keep me company in my kitchen, show my kids, and discover all the little secrets and tips that never quite make it to the written page. Fortunately, the kids have coaxed my mom into starring in her own cooking show.

A cookbook playdate with grandparents, cousins, aunts, uncles, or close friends can capture and preserve those memories, either on video or by watching and writing it all down for a more traditional cookbook. I recently visited my Aunt Linda and Uncle Roger in Texas and took copious notes for Linda's Ruggies (page 132) and Grandma Bea's Chopped String Beans (page 48) which I had lost the recipes for, but which I can now happily still make.

Have the older kids shoot the video and take notes. They can also take photographs to document the recipes. Younger ones can draw pictures. Everyone can start a recipe book in a three-ring binder. Have a binder for each child to take home. Include your signature recipe for them if you like.

I think comfort food is the best thing for a nostalgic playdate, so here are my suggestions for a menu devised around my family favorites.

MENU
- GRANDMA BEA'S CHOPPED STRING BEANS (PAGE 48)
- GRANDMA BEA'S BEEF AND BARLEY SOUP (PAGE 49)
- BACON-WRAPPED MEAT LOAF WITH SECRET SPINACH (PAGE 66) OR FANCY POT ROAST (PAGE 74)
- RUGGIES (AUNT LINDA'S RUGALACH) (PAGE 132)

CHAPTER 5 | **MAINS**

There are two ways to go when it comes to the main part of the meal: You can prepare an excellent cut of meat or fish, like a rack of ribs, or a grilled side of salmon and surround it with spectacular sides. Or you can prepare a standout dish, preferably one that can be put together in advance and cooked briefly in a hot oven before serving, like a parchment-baked fish.

Another tactic is to play around with the way you serve things—self-service is big in our house. A pot of chicken soup, or in the summer stacks of grilled burgers, are set alongside one enormous topping bar, so everyone can customize their bowl of soup or burger with a seemingly endless choice of both homemade and purchased toppings. You can make the preparation of the toppings as part of the playdate too.

If you have the time, double recipes and stash a batch in the freezer. Sometimes this becomes what I call a "dinner swap playdate" (page 84), where a few of us each make a double batch of a different main course and divide the spoils, so everyone gets to take home some food for the week. The extra effort feels minimal, the communal cooking is fun, and the kids can say they made dinner that week.

MINT TEA ROAST LAMB

Anya von Bremzen, my world traveler friend and cookbook author extraordinaire, provided a great solution for an Easter dinner that I was hosting at the last minute: a marinade made from mint tea bags. It's a smart way to deal with such a large amount of dried mint, and wacky enough to make you smile. I prefer peppermint to spearmint, but experiment—try a smoky Asian tea and serve with rice or use a fruit tea and serve with couscous. It's playful and seriously good, especially when served with Greek Roasted Potatoes (page 89) and Tangled Green Salad (page 95).

1 head garlic, cloves separated and peeled

⅓ cup mint tea (from about 10 bags)

1 tablespoon salt

1 tablespoon freshly ground pepper

Juice of 1 lemon

½ cup olive oil

One 6-pound leg of lamb, shank end

○ Preheat the oven to 425 degrees F.

○ Set half of the garlic cloves aside. Chop the remaining garlic half of cloves with a bit of salt to make a paste and transfer to a small bowl. (Or use a garlic press.) Crumble the mint between your fingers and add to the garlic. Add the salt, pepper, lemon juice, and while stirring, add enough of the oil to make a paste.

○ Cut the reserved cloves into slivers, put in a small bowl, and mix in a spoonful of the marinade to coat the slivers. Stud the lamb with the garlic slivers by making small slits all over the lamb with a sharp paring knife and slipping in the garlic. Spread the remaining marinade evenly over the lamb.

○ Place the lamb on a rack over a roasting pan or on a baking sheet and bake for 25 minutes. Turn the leg over and continue to roast until the internal temperature reaches 130 degrees F, about 30 to 35 minutes more. Allow the meat to rest on a cutting board for about 10 minutes before slicing, to allow the juices to settle.

SERVES 6

NOTE You can marinate the whole leg overnight; just wrap tightly in plastic and stash the lamb in the refrigerator. Remove the lamb from the fridge and let rest at room temperature for about 30 minutes before roasting.

○ **KIDS IN THE KITCHEN** ○

Most kids can help peel the garlic, and make the marinade by measuring, counting, and opening tea bags and crumbling the tea. Younger kids especially like to spread the marinade and stud the lamb with garlic slivers.

PARCHMENT-BAKED HALIBUT WITH SHIITAKES, LEMON, AND HERBS

This recipe has it all: it's healthful, beautiful, and a miniproject for the kids to prepare. It's been known to entice certain finicky eaters into—gasp!—trying a piece of fish, and maybe even a mushroom. I've simplified folding the parchment packages so they look like wrapped candies that the kids can make themselves. Set up an assembly line to make the packages, which can be done hours beforehand and refrigerated. Be adventurous. Follow the basic instructions, then vary the fish and flavorings. Try salmon fillets with halved cherry tomatoes, balsamic, and rosemary; snapper with orange slices and olives; or cod with peas, potatoes, and a mint sprig.

¼ pound shiitake mushrooms, stems removed

2 lemons, cut into 6 thin slices each, plus 1 tablespoon fresh lemon juice

Kosher salt and freshly ground pepper to taste

1½ tablespoons low-sodium soy sauce

1 tablespoon honey

1 tablespoon rice wine vinegar

Four 6-ounce skinless halibut fillets

Extra-virgin olive oil

4 sprigs fresh chervil, or 2 sprigs each fresh thyme and tarragon

SPECIAL EQUIPMENT: four 12-by-14-inch pieces of parchment paper, kitchen string

- Preheat the oven to 350 degrees F.

- In a medium bowl, toss the shiitakes with the lemon juice, salt, and pepper. Set aside.

- In a small bowl, mix together the soy, honey, and rice wine vinegar. Set aside.

- Season the fish with the salt and pepper. Lightly oil the parchment paper. Place an individual halibut fillet in the center of the paper. Spread 1 tablespoon of the soy and honey mixture on each fillet. Top with 3 lemon slices, and a quarter of the mushroom mixture and 1 chervil sprig (or half of a thyme and a tarragon sprig). Bring both sides of the paper together and fold. Continue folding the paper down until you reach the herbs. Take each end of the paper and twist them tightly, like a hard-candy wrapper. Make a little bow with kitchen string. Assemble the remaining 3 packets the same way.

- Place the packets on a sheet pan and bake for 10 to 12 minutes, until the packages puff up. Remove from the oven and serve immediately.

SERVES 4

SAFETY NOTE Make sure the little ones are not leaning closely over the packages when they are being opened as the little puff of steam can burn.

○ KIDS IN THE KITCHEN ○

The kids can do almost all of the work. Older kids should be supervised if cutting the lemons.

SHORT RIBS WITH CHOCOLATE, ORANGE, AND CINNAMON

This is my version of a dish I had over eighteen years ago when I was living in Spain, teaching English to corporate execs while knowing only minimal, tapas-bar Spanish myself. The ingredients are surprising—my children love adding the chocolate to the meat because they think it's really silly. The chocolate is not instantly identifiable, though, and your friends will be intrigued by the sophisticated play of flavors.

4 pounds short ribs, cut into
1½-by-4-inch pieces

1 teaspoon kosher salt

½ teaspoon freshly ground pepper

1 small orange, halved

3 sprigs fresh thyme

3 sprigs fresh parsley

1 bay leaf

¼ pound bacon (about 5 slices), cut
lengthwise into ¼-inch matchsticks

2 carrots, peeled and cut into small dice

1 celery stalk, cut into small dice

1 small onion, cut into small dice

3 cloves garlic, peeled

2 tablespoons all-purpose flour

1 tablespoon cocoa powder, plus more
for garnish

1 cup red wine

3 cups chicken or beef broth

○ Preheat the oven to 350 degrees F.

○ Season the short ribs with the salt and pepper. For a nicer presentation, tie each rib around the meat with kitchen string, like a package, so that they will stay on the bone during cooking. Set aside.

○ Remove the rind from one half of the orange; discard the pulp. Tie the thyme, parsley, bay leaf, and the piece of orange rind into a bundle with the kitchen string and set aside.

○ In a large Dutch oven set over medium-high heat, sauté the bacon, stirring frequently until the fat has rendered and the bacon is crisp. Remove from the pan, drain on a paper towel, and reserve.

○ Allow the fat to return to a sizzle and sear a few short ribs at a time over medium-high heat, taking care not to crowd the pan. (If they are crowded, the meat will steam and will not get that delicious, rich caramelization on the outside.) Sear the short ribs on all sides, about 1 to 2 minutes per side, taking care to regulate the heat so the drippings on the bottom of the pan don't burn. If the meat sticks to the pan, the rib is not ready to be turned. Place the seared ribs on a plate and drain the fat, leaving about 3 tablespoons in the pan.

NOTES To de-grease the sauce if you are serving the dish the same day, remove the ribs and transfer the sauce to a bowl. Set the bowl over a larger one filled with ice and a bit of water. Stir occasionally to cool the mixture to room temperature and place in the freezer. After about 20 minutes, the fat will congeal and you can remove it. Recombine ribs and sauce in the pot and reheat in a 350 degree F oven for 20 minutes, or on top of the stove.

A wonderful French pastry chef, Pierre Hermé, taught me to use a serrated knife to chop chocolate. I prefer an offset version, and bring the knife down at a slight angle to cut thin shards that melt quickly and evenly.

It's a fairly simple dish; the only really laborious and critical part is searing the ribs so you get a caramelized crust and lots of flavor in the sauce. Then you just throw everything else into the pot. Like so many braises, this dish is truly better the next day, freeing you up on the day of your get-together to even make dessert. A dusting of cocoa powder provides a hint to the mysterious flavor.

2 ounces bittersweet chocolate, finely chopped (see Notes)

1 small cinnamon stick, about 2 inches long

Mashed russet or sweet potatoes, noodles or rice for serving

SPECIAL EQUIPMENT: kitchen string

○ Add the carrots, celery, onion, and garlic, and sauté until the vegetables are softened and golden. Add the flour, and cook for about 30 seconds, stirring constantly so it does not burn. Add the cocoa powder and stir to coat the vegetables. Add the red wine, stir, and bring to a boil.

○ Return the bacon and seared ribs to the pan, and add the broth and bundle of herbs and orange rind. Bring the mixture to a boil, cover, and put in the oven for 1 hour. Add the grated chocolate and cinnamon stick, and continue to cook for another 1½ hours.

○ Cool the ribs to room temperature and chill overnight. (See Notes if serving the same day.) Remove the congealed fat from the top, and reheat in a preheated 350 degree F oven for about 45 minutes to 1 hour.

○ To serve, cut the strings from the ribs and remove the herb bundle. Taste the sauce and add additional salt or pepper if needed and a squeeze of orange juice. Arrange the ribs on a platter or individual plates with potatoes, noodles, or rice and dust with extra cocoa.

SERVES 4 GENEROUSLY

○ **KIDS IN THE KITCHEN** ○

Older kids can help tie the meat and peel the orange rind and chop the chocolate. Younger kids can measure and help add the chocolate into the hot pot while being supervised.

SLOW-COOKED SALMON WITH SALSA VERDE

Whether you grill your salmon or cook it low and slow in the oven as I explain below, this Italian green sauce is a breeze to make and takes plain fish into rarefied, "what was that recipe again?" status. I make a double batch and buy a little extra fish to toss with steamed potatoes for the next day's lunch. I find it calming to do all the chopping by hand, and older kids can practice their knife skills, but you can whiz it in the processor if you'd like; just add a third or so of the oil with the ingredients and drizzle in the rest. Remember, you want to keep the texture a bit coarse, so pulse carefully or you'll end up with green soup. The tangy sauce also enlivens cold roast pork or chicken breasts.

FOR THE SALSA VERDE

1 cup chopped flat-leaf parsley

1 cup chopped fresh mint leaves

2 cups fresh basil, cut into thin ribbons

1 cup extra virgin olive oil

4 cloves garlic, finely chopped

¼ cup capers, rinsed and chopped

6 anchovy fillets, soaked, bones removed, and chopped

2 tablespoons Dijon mustard

2 tablespoons red wine vinegar

⅛ teaspoon freshly ground pepper, or more to taste

Coarse sea salt, preferably Maldon

FOR THE SALMON

One 3-pound fillet center cut salmon

2 tablespoons extra virgin olive oil

½ teaspoon kosher salt

⅛ teaspoon freshly ground pepper

Lemon wedges for serving

- Mix all ingredients for the Salsa Verde in a small bowl. Add a pinch of salt and season to taste. Set aside until serving. Refrigerate if made earlier in the day and remove 1 hour or so before serving.

- Preheat the oven to 300 degrees F.

- To make the fish, coat it very lightly with extra virgin olive oil, season both sides with salt and pepper and place on a baking sheet skin side down. Cook for 24 to 28 minutes until the flesh is pink and just beyond translucent, or a few minutes longer if you prefer it well done. Remove the skin.

- To serve, place the whole piece of salmon on a platter, and top with the Salsa Verde, and surround with lemon wedges. Pass any additional sauce.

SERVES 4 TO 6

NOTE If you're grilling the salmon, coat and season as above, and place the fish on a medium-hot fire for 8 to 10 minutes, skin side down, with the lid closed. Do not turn the fish. Remove with a spatula, and don't worry if the piece breaks up. Arrange the chunks on a large platter. If the skin is not too charred you can leave it on the fish.

◦ KIDS IN THE KITCHEN ◦

An authentic Italian mezzaluna is a fun tool for older kids. This half-moon-shaped blade often comes with a wooden bowl to rock and chop, and can be used for the herbs. Or the older kids can learn the difference between bruising the herbs with a knife or cutting them correctly, slicing neatly through the leaves. Younger kids can measure and mix the salsa ingredients, and check the salmon for bones by lightly tracing fingers over its surface. They can also oil and season the fish, spoon the salsa over the cooked fish, and arrange the lemons on the platter.

BACON-WRAPPED MEAT LOAF WITH SECRET SPINACH

This is what I serve at Natasha's birthday party—it's the midwinter version of Mathias's summer birthday Burger Bar (see page 68). I borrowed a trick I learned at Martha Stewart to wrap the loaf with a bacon-and-sugary-mustard glaze, which distracts the kids from the wheat bread and spinach I sneak into my version. Use the shredding disc on your food processor for the onion, carrots, and even the garlic and parsley to speed things up. It might even help you sneak a few more healthful things past your pint-sized no-veggies police.

2 tablespoons olive oil

1 large yellow onion, peeled

2 carrots, peeled and finely grated

2 cloves garlic, peeled

One 10-ounce package frozen spinach, defrosted, drained, and coarsely chopped

3 slices whole wheat bread, crusts removed, cubed

½ cup milk

1 pound ground sirloin

¾ pound ground pork

2 large eggs

2 tablespoons chopped fresh parsley

2 tablespoons Dijon mustard

1 tablespoon kosher salt

1½ teaspoons freshly ground pepper

2 teaspoons tomato paste

¾ cup packed light brown sugar

1½ tablespoons ground yellow mustard, preferably Coleman's

½ pound sliced smoked bacon

○ Preheat the oven to 375 degrees F.

○ Shred the onion, carrots, and garlic in a food processor using a shredding disc, or grate by hand.

○ Heat the olive oil in a large sauté pan over medium-high heat, and add the onion, carrots, garlic, and spinach and sauté until the vegetables are softened, about 4 minutes. Transfer to a large bowl and set aside until slightly cool.

○ Meanwhile, in a small bowl, soak the bread in the milk for 5 minutes. Add the bread and milk mixture to the cooled vegetables, and add the ground sirloin, ground pork, eggs, parsley, Dijon mustard, salt, and pepper. Using your hands, gently combine, breaking up the bread chunks and distributing the seasonings evenly.

○ Put the mixture in a large ungreased baking dish or roasting pan. Shape into a 5-by-12-inch loaf. In a small bowl, mix the tomato paste, brown sugar, ground mustard, and a few tablespoons of warm water. Brush the meat loaf all over with half of the glaze.

○ Overlap bacon slices across the top, covering the meat, and brush with the remaining glaze.

○ Bake the meat loaf, brushing halfway through cooking time with any remaining glaze, until the juices run clear when the loaf is pierced and the bacon is crisp, about 50 minutes. A meat thermometer inserted in the middle should read 155 degrees F. Let cool 10 minutes before slicing.

SERVES 6 TO 8

NOTE For parties, make the meat loaf in minimuffin or loaf pans, trimming the bacon to size with kitchen shears. Test for doneness after 40 minutes.

○ **KIDS IN THE KITCHEN** ○

Kids can help peel carrots, and older ones can help with the chopping and measuring. Younger ones love to cut the crusts off with a plastic knife and soak the bread in the milk. All kids can mix the meat loaf, help shape it, make the glaze, glaze the meat loaf, and layer with the bacon.

300-DEGREE PORK ROAST

I think a roast pork loin is the perfect Sunday supper. After you're done with a fabulous dinner, the leftovers make delicious weekday sandwiches when thinly sliced and spread with jam and more mustard or pesto. My kids prefer this to sliced turkey. The roast should be crisp outside and juicy inside, which is why I start by searing it in the pan on the stove top and then finish it in a slow oven. This roast is a great reason to invest in an instant-read thermometer if you don't already have one. Your oven timer just isn't going to cut it if you want that juicy, perfectly cooked pork. Serve with Dad's Campfire Potatoes (page 91) or Broccoli Rabe (page 108).

One 3-pound pork roast, boneless
½ teaspoon salt
¼ teaspoon freshly ground pepper
2 tablespoons Dijon mustard
1 clove garlic, finally chopped
3 tablespoons finely chopped fresh tarragon
2 tablespoons olive oil

○ Preheat the oven to 300 degrees F.

○ Season the pork with the salt and pepper and let sit at room temperature for about 15 minutes before cooking. In a small bowl, mix the mustard, garlic, and tarragon and set aside.

○ Select an ovenproof 12- to 14-inch sauté pan. If the pork is too large for your pan, place a roasting pan over two burners.

○ Heat the oil in the pan over medium-high heat until the oil is shimmering. Put the pork, fat side down, into the oil and cook until the fat is crisp and golden brown, about 5 minutes. Turn the pork and cook for an additional 3 minutes. Turn off the heat and carefully transfer the roast to a cutting board.

○ Allow the pork to cool slightly, and spread the mustard mixture over the entire roast. Drain the fat from the pan. Return the roast to the pan and cook for 55 to 65 minutes, or until an instant-read thermometer reads between 145 and 150 degrees F. Allow the roast to sit for 10 minutes, and carve into thin slices.

SERVES 6

NOTES Bone-in roasts are more flavorful, but can be tricky to find. If your butcher has one, by all means buy it, but ask for a 4- to 5-pound roast to compensate for the bone weight. Use the instant-read thermometer because the cooking time may vary.

You can substitute fresh rosemary for the tarragon.

○ **KIDS IN THE KITCHEN** ○

Kids of any age can season the cold roast and prepare the mustard mixture. Let the older kids practice carving.

The world of kids' birthday parties is a thrilling mixture of madness, excess, and sheer joy. Even so, I still like to keep them as homey as possible, and these two seasonal menus really help: the Burger Bar for Mathias's summer birthday and comfort foods and spectacular cake for our winter baby, Natasha. They've actually become family traditions.

SUMMER BIRTHDAY COOKOUT

This was a little easier when we had a house in the suburbs. Now I have to scramble a bit to reserve space in the park, but it's just as much fun. Make sure to ask a relative or a few friends to man the grill, and stock it with a mix of hamburgers, turkey burgers, and veggie burgers. If you have some extra grill space, serve ears of corn. The toppings are a mix of the kid-friendly familiar, and the slightly more exotic to entertain the adults. Pile the table high with as many of these toppings as you have time to prepare (most can be made at least a day in advance), and don't be afraid to fill out the spread with salads from your local deli. Pack an ice cooler if you're carrying the cake to the park.

BURGER BAR

- GRILLED HAMBURGERS AND TURKEY AND VEGGIE BURGERS
  TOPPINGS Sugar-and-Spice Bacon (page 165), chipotle mayonnaise (recipe follows), pineapple and mango salsa (recipe follows), marinated feta cheese, crumbled Maytag Blue Cheese, sliced Cheddar, ketchup, mustard, pickles, sliced red onion, tomatoes, shredded lettuce

- SWEET POTATO SALAD WITH LIME AND ANCHO (PAGE 96)

- CILANTRO SLAW, ASIAN RADICCHIO SLAW (PAGE 99), OR SPICY SLAW (PAGE 97)

- GRILLED CORN

- HOMEMADE ICE CREAM CAKE (PAGE 147)

- STRAWBERRY LEMONADE

- CHIPOTLE MAYONNAISE: Chop 1 teaspoon or more (to taste) of canned chipotles in sauce into 2 cups mayonnaise.

- PINEAPPLE AND MANGO SALSA: Cut 1 pineapple and 1 mango into ¼ inch dice. Add 1 finely diced red onion, 1 diced jalapeño and ⅓ cup chopped cilantro. Add zest and juice of 1 lime and ½ teaspoon salt and a few grindings of fresh pepper and stir to combine. Can be made the night before if kept refrigerated.

- MARINATED FETA CHEESE: Crumble 1 pound of feta with ¼ teaspoon red pepper flakes, 1 teaspoon dried oregano, and zest and juice of 1 lemon. Toss with ½ cup of olive oil.

WINTER FAIRY-TALE BIRTHDAY / CUPCAKE DECORATING

This menu was designed to coax friends out of their cold-weather cocoons. Since it's too chilly to grill, the Bacon-Wrapped Meat Loaf with Secret Spinach (page 66) brings smiles to snow bunnies. If the crowd is small, you can bake the mixture in muffin cups or mini loaf pans and cut the bacon with scissors to fit. Warm the cider and serve with individual cinnamon sticks, or fill pitchers with cold apple cider and apple slices.

The Fairy-Tale Birthday Cake will enchant everyone and comes with a cupcake decorating activity. Just bake an extra batch of plain cupcakes and provide an array of colored whipped cream frosting and decorating sugars. Fill the favor bags with decorating sugars, snowflakes, and small dolls. And don't miss the chocolate "Danger Mountain" variation (page 129) for your young adventurers.

WINTER FAIRY-TALE BIRTHDAY MENU

- GRANDMA BEA'S CHOPPED STRING BEANS (PAGE 48)
- BACON-WRAPPED MEAT LOAF WITH SECRET SPINACH (PAGE 66)
- SWEET POTATO SALAD WITH LIME AND ANCHO (PAGE 96) OR MASHED POTATOES
- SNOW WHITE'S SALAD (PAGE 105)
- WARM APPLE CIDER WITH CINNAMON STICKS
- FAIRY-TALE BIRTHDAY CAKE (PAGE 127)
- CUPCAKES FOR DECORATING

FRIDGE RIBS

Sometimes, when a recipe crisis arises you have to just wing it. As these ribs show, that sort of culinary improv can really pay off. They've become one of my husband's favorite dishes, and they were a complete fluke. We were at my brother's house, and I had prepared a spice rub that was too hot for human consumption. I had to quickly change course if there was to be any hope of getting dinner on the table. I literally emptied the contents of my brother's fridge, did a little inspired mixing, and voila! Now it's a weekend family favorite, especially after I learned that marinating the ribs overnight really improves the flavor. Serve with Sesame Orzo with Dried Apricots, Currants, and Slivered Almonds (page 111) or Sweet Potato Salad with Lime and Ancho (page 96).

FOR THE MARINADE

1 cup soy sauce

1 tablespoon toasted sesame oil

½ cup apricot jam

½ teaspoon ground coriander

½ teaspoon ground cinnamon

¼ teaspoon freshly ground pepper

2 teaspoons chopped garlic

One 3-inch piece fresh ginger, peeled and grated

¼ cup white wine

½ cup honey, plus additional honey for basting

5 pounds pork spareribs (not baby back)

○ Mix all marinade ingredients together and pour over ribs. Place in roasting pan, cover with foil, and refrigerate. Let marinate at least 3 hours, or, even better, overnight.

○ Preheat the oven to 325 degrees F.

○ Remove the ribs from the refrigerator and let sit at room temperature for 15 minutes. Place the ribs, still covered with foil, in the oven. Bake for 2½ hours, or until the meat is tender. Set the oven to broil, and raise the rack as necessary. Drizzle a few tablespoons of honey evenly over the ribs and broil until slightly crisp, about 2 to 3 minutes.

○ Or, finish the ribs on the grill: prepare a medium-hot fire, and remove the ribs from the oven after 2 hours. Drizzle with honey and cook until slightly charred, about 5 to 10 minutes per side.

○ Allow the ribs to rest for 5 minutes, cut between the bones to separate them, and serve.

SERVES 4

NOTE A microplaner is the best tool for grating the ginger quickly and evenly if you don't have a special ginger grater.

○ **KIDS IN THE KITCHEN** ○

With careful supervision, most kids can begin to grate the ginger for an inch or so, and they can measure the marinade ingredients and spread the marinade on the ribs.

CHINATOWN ROAST PORK

Pork tenderloin is a really versatile meat, and it's worth keeping a stash in the freezer. You can grill or roast them and serve with everything from corn salsa to mashed potatoes. My kids love this Asian version, served with the Sesame Orzo with Dried Apricots, Currants, and Slivered Almonds (page 111), and Asian Radicchio Slaw (page 99), or with a frozen veggie stir-fry. You can easily double the recipe and chop up the leftovers to perk up some homemade fried rice for the next day's lunch.

The pork needs to marinate for 2 days, so I like to get it started on a Friday night and serve it for Sunday dinner. It reminds me of my family's Sunday night visits to New York's Chinatown when I was growing up.

FOR THE MARINADE

½ cup maple syrup (see Notes)

1 carrot, washed and cut into medium dice

1 small onion, cut into medium dice

One 2-inch chunk fresh ginger, peeled and finely chopped

6 cloves garlic, finely chopped

¼ cup coarsely chopped fresh cilantro leaves and stems

1 teaspoon crushed black pepper, or ½ teaspoon coarsely ground pepper

1 tablespoon dry sherry or Marsala wine

1 tablespoon toasted sesame oil

¼ cup soy sauce

2 tablespoons salt

One 1-pound pork tenderloin

3 tablespoons maple syrup

Orzo or rice for serving

○ In a medium bowl, mix all marinade ingredients together. Place the pork loin in a sturdy plastic zip bag or an airtight container, pour in the marinade, and seal or cover tightly. Marinate in the refrigerator for 2 days.

○ Preheat the oven to 375 degrees F.

○ Remove the pork from the marinade and reserve the marinade. Brush the tenderloin with the 3 tablespoons maple syrup and roast on a baking sheet or shallow roasting pan for 45 minutes.

○ Meanwhile, strain the reserved marinade into a small saucepan. Bring the marinade to a boil over medium-high heat and continue boiling to reduce until syrupy, about 3 minutes.

○ Let the tenderloin rest for 5 minutes and slice thinly on an angle. Serve with orzo or rice and serve with reduced sauce.

SERVES 4

NOTES Use Grade B maple syrup; the flavor is stronger, and it is less expensive.

In warmer weather, grill the pork over a medium-hot fire, about 15 minutes per side.

○ **KIDS IN THE KITCHEN** ○

Older kids can cut the vegetables under supervision; younger ones can measure and mix the marinade.

DUCK AND ANDOUILLE JAMBALAYA

New Orleans has been a dear place to me over the last eighteen years. Anthony proposed to me there after we feasted on oysters at Casamento's. I started cooking school, and a few years later I became the first sous chef at the Food Network, where Emeril taught me a few tricks with the flavors of that city. Eventually, I met the city's best cooks and artisans while shooting some shows there with Martha Stewart.

This dish is ideal for a crowd, and it's really not as much work as it seems. Just read through the recipe a few times and have everything organized. Use a roasting pan set over two burners, rather than a deep pot, so the rice doesn't become mushy. If your kids are like mine and don't adore spicy food, just roast a plain piece of duck for them.

2 to 4 tablespoons Cajun spice blend

2 ducks (about 5 pounds each) cut into 8 pieces, or 10 pounds cut-up chicken (see Notes)

2 tablespoons vegetable oil

2 pounds spicy andouille sausage or a milder smoked sausage such as kielbasa, thinly sliced

4 cups chopped onions

2 cups chopped green bell pepper

1 cup chopped celery

3 teaspoons kosher salt

½ teaspoon freshly ground black pepper

5 bay leaves

4 cups seeded and chopped tomatoes, fresh or canned

2 tablespoons chopped garlic

4 cups white rice

7 cups chicken stock

1½ cups chopped scallions

○ Preheat the oven to 375 degrees F.

○ Rub the Cajun spice blend into the skin of the duck. Heat the vegetable oil in a roasting pan that will fit over two burners, set over medium-high heat. Sear the duck, skin side down, for about 5 minutes, until the skin is crisp and browned. Turn and sear the other side for 4 to 5 minutes. Transfer the duck to a rimmed baking sheet or another roasting pan and set aside.

○ Carefully drain all but about ¼ cup of the duck fat from the pan. Return the pan to medium-high heat, add the sausage, and sauté for 2 to 4 minutes, or until golden brown. Add the onions, peppers, and celery to the pan, and season with salt and pepper.

○ Sauté the vegetables for about 5 minutes, or until soft and light golden brown. Add the bay leaves, tomatoes, and garlic, and sauté for 2 more minutes. Stir in the rice and sauté for 2 minutes, stirring frequently. Add the chicken stock.

○ Bring the liquid to a boil, and then reduce to a gentle simmer. Cover the pan with aluminum foil and cook the jambalaya for 25 to 30 minutes, until the rice is fully cooked.

○ Meanwhile, place the duck in the oven and roast for 10 to 15 minutes, until the dark-meat juices run clear and are no longer pink. The breast meat should be slightly pink. Remove the pieces from the oven as they are cooked through.

○ Remove the foil from the rice, stir in the scallions and taste for seasoning. Transfer the rice mixture to a large platter, and arrange the duck over the rice, or arrange the jambalaya on individual plates.

SERVES 8 TO 10

NOTES If your supermarket won't cut up the duck for you, buy an equal weight of duck breasts, legs, and thighs. D'Artagnan sells these vacuum-sealed (see Sources on page 173). Or substitute 2 cut-up chickens.

To make ahead, cook the rice for three-quarters of the suggested cooking time. Reheat, uncovered, in the oven the next day at 375 degrees F. If you like the rice really crunchy, you can turn up the heat a bit in the oven.

◦ KIDS IN THE KITCHEN ◦

My kids love to identify the duck parts as I cut them. They can also rub in the spice mixture, but be careful to avoid contact with the eyes. Older kids can help prepare the vegetables and measure.

FANCY POT ROAST

This is comfort food with an unexpected twist—the celery root is guaranteed to keep all the kids and most adults guessing. It provides the tang of celery with more creaminess and a truly gnarly appearance to amuse the kids.

Since this simmers for a bit, I've devised a snack for hungry kids. When I prep the potatoes, I peel them with a paring knife so some extra potato clings to the skin. Then I toss them with olive oil and salt and roast in a 400 degree F oven till they're crispy. Like any pot roast, this just gets better the next day. Serve with Snow White's Salad (page 105).

One 2-pound boneless chuck roast

2 teaspoons kosher salt

½ teaspoon freshly ground pepper

2 tablespoons olive oil

1 sweet onion, thinly sliced

5 cloves garlic, peeled

4 cups (total) red wine and beef stock, or all beef stock

1 large celeriac (celery root) (about 1 pound), peeled (see Note)

3 to 4 Yukon Gold potatoes (about 1½ pounds), peeled and cut into chunks

½ pound (about 1½ cups) baby carrots

4 sprigs fresh thyme

4 to 6 sprigs fresh parsley

○ Preheat oven to 325 degrees F.

○ Season the roast liberally with the salt and pepper on all sides. Heat the oil in a large Dutch oven over medium-high heat, and sear each side of the roast until dark golden brown, about 3 to 5 minutes for the first side, and 2 to 3 minutes for each remaining side.

○ Remove the roast to a plate. Reduce the heat slightly, add the onion and garlic, and sauté until softened and golden. Add 1 cup of the liquid and bring to a boil, scraping the browned bits from the bottom of the pan. Return the roast and any drippings to the pot. Add remaining vegetables, herbs, and liquid. Cover and bake for 3½ to 4 hours, until the meat is tender.

○ If you are serving the same day, strain the sauce into a bowl without crushing the vegetables, and set the bowl over a larger one filled with ice and a bit of water. Stir occasionally to cool the mixture to room temperature and place the sauce in the freezer. After about 20 minutes, remove the bowl from the freezer and discard the layer of chilled fat. Return the sauce, vegetables, and the meat to the pot and return to the oven, until warm. Or chill overnight and remove the fat that hardens on top. Reheat in the oven, slice the meat, and serve with the vegetables.

○ If you prefer a slightly thicker sauce, transfer the sauce to a wide saucepan and boil until thickened. Or dissolve a generous teaspoon of cornstarch into cold water, add the mixture to the sauce, and simmer to thicken. Do not boil.

○ Serve with Dijon mustard drizzled on top.

SERVES 4

NOTE Don't be put off by celeriac's thick skin; treat it like a pineapple. Just slice off the top and bottom so it sits squarely on the cutting board, and use your knife to cut away the sides from top to bottom.

○ KIDS IN THE KITCHEN ○

Kids of all ages can help season the roast and older ones can peel garlic, and peel the potatoes with a peeler if not making "fries." They can also help measure.

FROM THE FREEZER

My husband fears my freezer, while I consider it my best friend. Yes, it's bursting, and could be better organized, but it's all buried treasure to me. I consider the freezer an extension of my pantry. In addition to the dishes that freeze well, there's an arsenal of ingredients that I whip into quick pasta sauces, dips, desserts, and even drinks.

BACON AND PANCETTA Bacon is Mathias's favorite food. I am always looking for a new variety for curling into flowers for breakfast, topping meat loaf, or sugaring with cayenne for burgers (www.gratefulpalate.com even has a bacon-of-the-month club). My favorite brands include Nodine's and Nueske. I keep a hunk of Niman Ranch pancetta for Anthony's Spaghetti Carbonara (page 79).

BERRIES I buy frozen berries (unsweetened, not in syrup) at the supermarket. In the summer, if we've gone crazy at a U-pick farm, we wash and dry them, spread them out on lined trays, freeze them individually, and then transfer the frozen berries to larger freezer bags. We use them for smoothies (see page 167) and granitas.

BUTTER I always have at least two pounds of unsalted butter for baking. The kids also like to blend a stick with some honey or a few spoonfuls of jam for toast or pancakes. If it's a long rainy day and I need a project, we fill little silicone molds and chill them.

FROZEN ARTICHOKE HEARTS For bruschetta, I defrost them and toss them with oil, lemon wedges, and herbs, then roast for 15 to 20 minutes in a 400 degree F oven. For a dip I whiz them with goat cheese and a splash of olive oil and some fresh herbs. And they make a sophisticated pizza topping (see page 51).

MINT CUBES See page 52.

NUTS A corner of the freezer is devoted to bagged nuts for cooking, baking, or snacking. I toast sliced, blanched almonds and toss them with egg whites and sugar, then spread on top of cakes before baking. Slivered, blanched almonds add crunch to salads or pulsed into flour for cakes or tarts. Salted and fried Marcona almonds from Spain are for nibbling (these rarely make it into the freezer as they are eaten immediately). Whole pistachios are a fast way to fill out a spread of cheese and crackers, or for tossing into orzo or green salads, or even chicken salads. Pecan and walnut halves are good for candying (see page 33), make a crunchy crust for a linzertorte (see page 119), or a quick batch of shortbread—either sweet with brown sugar, or with fresh rosemary for a savory version. Pulse almonds with arugula (see page 77) or for traditional basil pesto or add a handful to salads and pastas.

PIZZA DOUGH I find store-bought dough from the freezer section or purchased fresh and frozen from the local parlor indispensable, and have included recipes (see page 50).

PUFF PASTRY Dufour or Pepperidge Farm from the freezer section is great for tarts (see page 39), quick desserts, or easy cheese sticks and for encasing sausages or franks.

RUBBED PORK RIBS Rub your favorite spice rub over a rack of pork ribs, wrap carefully, and freeze. Defrost overnight in the fridge and bake slowly (see Fridge Ribs, page 70), then finish on the grill for a lazy main course.

ARUGULA-ALMOND PESTO WITH PASTA AND GRILLED SHRIMP

This basil-less take on pesto is a standard from my catering days. It's even easier to make now that prewashed baby arugula is available in the salad section of many supermarkets. The almonds add a sweet counterpoint to the peppery arugula and the finished dish is beautifully bright and colorful. I usually throw in a tubular pasta like rigatoni or penne rigate because the ridges catch the pesto really well, but when I make this for my kids, I use regular spaghetti so my son can pretend he's eating green worms. Substitute grilled chicken for the shrimp if you like. Be sure to check the seasoning carefully at the end, adding extra salt or lemon to brighten the flavors and make the dish sing. It's great cold, too—in fact, I actually prefer it that way.

One 5-ounce package washed baby arugula (about 4 cups)

½ cup blanched almonds

Juice of 1½ lemons

1 clove garlic

2 teaspoons kosher salt

½ teaspoon freshly ground pepper

1½ cups extra-virgin olive oil

½ cup grated Parmesan cheese, plus extra for serving

1 pound uncooked rigatoni, penne rigate, or spaghetti

1 pound large shrimp (13 to 15 per pound), peeled, deveined, with tails left on

1 cup pear or cherry tomatoes, halved, tossed with ¼ teaspoon salt

SPECIAL EQUIPMENT: wooden skewers

○ In the bowl of a food processor, combine the arugula, almonds, lemon juice, garlic, 1 teaspoon of the salt, the pepper, and ¾ cup of the oil. Process while pouring another ½ cup of oil in a thin stream through the tube of the processor. The pesto should be a medium-fine consistency. Stir in the cheese.

○ Bring a large pot of water to a boil. Prepare a hot grill, or preheat a cast-iron grill pan or the broiler. While the grill heats, soak the skewers so they do not burn on the grill.

○ Cook the pasta until *al dente*, tender but slightly firm, according to the directions on the package. Toss the shrimp with the remaining ¼ cup of olive oil and the remaining 1 teaspoon of salt and a few more grindings of fresh pepper. If grilling, skewer the shrimp for easy handling; if broiling, place directly on a baking sheet.

○ Grill or broil the shrimp for 1 to 2 minutes per side, until pink and cooked through when tested with the tip of a knife.

○ Toss the hot pasta with the pesto. Add the cherry tomatoes, and a bit more oil if the pesto is a bit dry, and toss. Arrange in individual bowls or on a platter and top with the grilled shrimp. Sprinkle with coarse salt and additional fresh pepper to taste. Add a squeeze of lemon, and serve.

SERVES 4 TO 6

○ **KIDS IN THE KITCHEN** ○

Older kids can help peel, devein, and skewer the shrimp, and halve tomatoes, with supervision. Younger kids can juice lemons, measure, pour oil through the feed tube, soak skewers, garnish, and arrange plates.

GRILLED LOBSTERS WITH GARLIC BUTTER

My mother is the most devoted lobster eater on the planet. A visit to her house on Long Island invariably means a trip to the lobster farm for our Saturday night supper of grilled lobsters and local corn. My passion for that crustacean isn't far behind hers: My brother still talks about how we insisted on lobster rolls for breakfast during our visits when he lived in Maine.

Admittedly, this recipe is not for the squeamish: You need to pith—that's a euphemism for kill (sorry!)—the live lobsters and then split them in half. That is the most humane way to do it, as I learned when I was asked to prep the lobsters for the more soft-hearted chefs at the Food Network. I've also provided an alternative method, but note that the cooking time varies, depending on which method you have used.

½ cup (1 stick) butter, melted

1 tablespoon finely chopped garlic

Juice of 1 lemon

½ teaspoon salt

⅛ teaspoon freshly ground pepper

Four 1¾ pound lobsters (see Note)

○ Prepare a medium-hot grill.

○ Melt the butter with the garlic, lemon juice, and salt and pepper. Set aside.

○ If possible, fit a cutting board across the sink; this is the easiest way to handle the mess. If that is awkward, place 1 lobster on the cutting board at a time. If you have time, freeze the lobster for 15 minutes to relax the nervous system. You will have less wriggling on the cutting board. Locate the crease at the back of the neck just beneath the eyes. Plunge the knife tip halfway through the lobster. Remove the knife and turn the lobster over. Cut the lobster down the middle, slicing through the clear shell covering the tail, but do not slice through the outer shell. Slightly crack the claws with the back of the knife.

○ Alternatively, bring a large pot of water and 1 tablespoon of salt to a boil. Add 1 or 2 lobsters at a time, and parboil until the shells just begin to turn red, about 3 minutes. Remove and let cool slightly. Split the lobsters as described above.

○ Brush the lobster flesh with the butter mixture, and brush the butter mixture into the claw cracks. Place the lobster, shell side down, on the grill rack; cover the grill and cook for 10 to 12 minutes (7 to 8 minutes if you parboiled the lobsters), basting every 3 minutes or so. To check for doneness, poke at the tail with the point of a knife; the meat should be white and opaque.

SERVES 4

NOTE Buy the lobsters on the day you will cook them, and store them in paper bags—not plastic—in a bowl in the refrigerator until you are ready to cook.

○ **KIDS IN THE KITCHEN** ○

Gauge your child (and their friends) before trying this one. Some find this traumatic, although this is a good time to discuss where our food really comes from. The G-rated tasks include making the garlic butter and squeezing the lemon.

SPAGHETTI CARBONARA

This is my husband Anthony's definition of comfort food. (And don't let his name mislead you; he's not Italian.) It's a creamy, salty, soothing melange that makes a perfect late dinner on a Friday, after a hard week. We eat half, and I cook the leftovers like a pancake in a bit of olive oil for the kids' lunch the next day (see Note). Unless it's been a *really* bad week and we finish the whole bowl ourselves.

If you're making a big batch, cook the pancetta and onion ahead of time, and rewarm them in the pan while the spaghetti cooks. If you can get organic or local farm eggs, use them. You can really taste the difference.

2 tablespoons kosher salt

½ pound pancetta or good bacon

1 small sweet onion, chopped

1 cup grated Pecorino Romano cheese

4 eggs

¼ teaspoon freshly ground black pepper

1 pound uncooked spaghetti

○ Bring a large pot of water to a boil and add the salt.

○ In a large (12- to 14-inch) sauté the pan over medium-high heat, sauté pancetta and onion until crispy and golden. Do not drain the fat from the pan, but remove the pan from the heat while spaghetti is cooked.

○ In a large measuring cup or small bowl, mix the cheese, eggs, and pepper and set aside.

○ Cook the spaghetti according to the package directions until *al dente*, tender but slightly firm. Drain the pasta and reserve ¼ cup of the pasta-cooking water.

○ Rewarm the pancetta mixture in the sauté pan over medium heat, and add the cooked spaghetti and the reserved cooking water. Using tongs or two wooden spoons, toss the pasta until most of the water is absorbed.

○ Transfer the pasta to a large bowl, and quickly stir in the cheese and egg mixture, tossing well. Taste for seasoning and add a sprinkle of salt if needed. Divide the pasta among warmed serving bowls and top with more grated cheese and freshly ground pepper. Serve immediately.

SERVES 4

NOTES If you are concerned about the health risks of raw eggs for younger children or a pregnant friend, skip them. Simply set aside their portions of both the pasta and pancetta mixture before adding the egg mixture. Toss the reserved portions with a bit of butter and grated cheese and serve.

To make a pancake out of any leftovers, heat a few tablespoons of olive oil in a nonstick sauté pan, and add any leftover pasta, flattening the pasta mixture with a spatula to form a pancake. Cook until crispy, about 3 to 4 minutes; flip the pancake; and cook until crispy and warm inside, about 3 minutes more.

○ **KIDS IN THE KITCHEN** ○

Kids of almost any age can help add the salt to the cold water, crack the eggs, help toss, and add extra cheese and pepper.

BAKED RIGATONI WITH SAUSAGE, BUTTERNUT SQUASH, AND KALE

This is a rich dish—cold-weather comfort food at its best. It's a great way to get the kids to eat their vegetables: they'll like the mac-and-cheese feel, and you'll like the fact that they're eating something new. At a quick glance, the recipe may seem complicated, but it is really just a few well-choreographed steps. Read through it first to get the rhythm. The key is to be organized—set the water up to boil first, preheat the oven for the squash, and then start to sauté the sausage. It comes together very quickly. The best part is that you can assemble this dish a day in advance and simply bake it the next day.

1½ pounds butternut squash, peeled and cut into 2-inch chunks

4 tablespoons olive oil

6 to 8 sprigs fresh thyme

6 cloves garlic, peeled

1 teaspoon kosher salt, plus extra for seasoning

½ teaspoon freshly ground pepper, plus extra for seasoning

1 pound Italian sweet fennel sausage links, removed from casings

1 bunch of lacinato or black or dinosaur kale, carefully washed, tough stems removed, and roughly chopped (see Note)

¾ pound rigatoni

2 cups heavy cream

1¾ cups finely grated Pecorino Romano cheese

½ cup breadcrumbs

○ Bring a large pot of water to a boil for the pasta.

○ Preheat the oven to 400 degrees F.

○ Lightly oil or butter a 9-by-13-inch gratin or baking dish.

○ On a large baking sheet or in a roasting pan, toss the squash with 3 tablespoons of the olive oil. Scatter the thyme sprigs and 3 of the garlic cloves over the squash. Season with salt and pepper. Roast in the oven for about 20 to 25 minutes, until the squash is tender, but not mushy. Reduce the oven to 375 degrees F.

○ Heat the remaining tablespoon of the oil in a large Dutch oven set over medium-high heat. Add the sausage and cook, stirring frequently, until the meat is fully cooked and no longer pink. Remove the sausage with a slotted spoon, and put it in a large bowl. Drain most of the oil, leaving about 2 tablespoons in the pan. Lower heat to medium, add the kale and remaining 3 garlic cloves and sauté for 3 to 5 minutes, until the kale is wilted. If it begins to burn or stick add a few tablespoons of water. Season lightly with salt and pepper. Turn off the heat, remove the garlic, and add the kale to the sausage in the large bowl.

○ When the squash has finished cooking, remove from the oven. Remove the garlic and thyme sprigs (some of the herb will stick to the squash, which is fine), and add the squash to the sausage mixture.

○ Cook the pasta, and drain about 2 minutes before the package directions suggest, so the pasta is still a bit firm. It will finish cooking in the oven.

➡ CONTINUED

➡ **CONTINUED**

○ Toss the drained pasta with the sausage mixture. Add the cream, 1½ cups of the grated cheese, and 1 teaspoon salt and ½ teaspoon pepper. Toss gently. Transfer to a gratin or baking dish, and top with the breadcrumbs and the remaining ¼ cup of grated cheese.

(If you are making this in advance, allow the mixture to cool to room temperature, cover with plastic wrap, and place in the refrigerator.)

○ Bake for 25 minutes, until heated through and crusty on top.

SERVES 6

NOTE I love the nutty flavor of the lacinato kale, but you can use any kale available, Swiss chard, or even frozen spinach. Look for precut fresh butternut squash at the store to make things even easier.

○ **KIDS IN THE KITCHEN** ○

Kids of all ages can help prepare the baking dish, wash kale, peel garlic, measure, toss squash with oil and herbs, and top with breadcrumbs and cheese. Older kids can grate the cheese.

PARMESAN CHICKEN FINGERS

This grown-up version of chicken nuggets was inspired by a buttery dish my friend Pino Luongo, the Tuscan genius, served me at his New York City restaurant. He has banished the breadcrumbs, and I have followed his example. My version uses a bit of self-rising flour to make a light, cheesy crust. Serve them alone as a great finger food; skewered, with slices of lemon; or for a little taste of summer year-round, topped with a bit of arugula and an easy cherry tomato salad. Here's where the flexible plastic spatula shines—use it to scrape up the cheese that sticks to the pan. This is best made with Parmigiano-Reggiano that's been pulsed in the food processor, for a thick, pebbly crust.

¼ teaspoon kosher salt

⅛ teaspoon freshly ground pepper

½ cup self-rising cake flour (see Notes)

1 egg

⅓ pound Parmesan cheese, grated
(see Notes)

1 pound chicken tenders (see Notes)

¼ cup olive oil

3 tablespoons butter

2 lemons, quartered

◎ Preheat the oven to 300 degrees F.

◎ In a shallow bowl or plate, combine the salt and pepper with the flour. Beat the egg in another shallow bowl, and put the cheese in third shallow plate. Dredge the chicken tenders in the flour and pat off the excess. Dip in the egg and let the excess drain. Dredge the tenders in the cheese, covering both sides evenly and pressing firmly so the cheese adheres. Dredge the remaining tenders in the same way.

◎ Heat 2 tablespoons of the olive oil and 1 tablespoon of the butter in a nonstick skillet over high heat until bubbling. Add a few pieces of chicken and cook for about 2 to 3 minutes per side. Place chicken on a baking sheet and keep warm in oven. Continue cooking until all the chicken is done, wiping the pan as needed and adding additional oil and butter. If the cheese is getting too dark, readjust the heat.

◎ Serve on a platter, skewered with lemon wedges, and if desired top with arugula and Balsamic Cherry Tomato Salad (page 104).

SERVES 4

NOTES The tenders can be sautéed in advance and re-warmed in a 300 degree F oven for 15 minutes.

You can really taste the difference if you use true Parmigiano-Reggiano cheese. Remove the rind, cut into chunks, and drop these down a food processor tube (using the metal blade) while the machine is running. Or buy grated cheese from the cheese counter at the cheese shop or the deli counter at the supermarket, but avoid those tired cans.

Self-rising cake flour makes the crust a bit lighter. If you don't have any, add ¾ teaspoon baking powder and ¼ teaspoon more salt to the all-purpose flour.

◦ KIDS IN THE KITCHEN ◦

Controlled chaos is the goal here. Let the kids measure and dredge, while explaining the importance of proper dredging so the chicken doesn't become gummy. As chicken fingers tend to be sacred they might just listen. And let them plate the fingers with the salad, it might coax them into eating more of it.

This is a great way to spend a Sunday and tackle the anxiety associated with getting dinner on the table every weeknight. It's also a fun way to hang out in the kitchen with a couple of friends. A total of three seems to work best. The week before, pick the friend with the best kitchen to be the host. Choose one main dish recipe per person. On the day of the playdate, each parent can bring any special equipment and her own ingredients, or the host or whoever had the easiest week can do the shopping and split the bill. Each parent makes a triple-size batch of one recipe and then divvies them up, and, voila, dinner for three nights of the week!

It gets pretty crowded and chaotic, so this tends to be less of a hands-on playdate and more of a grown-up activity. At least some of the prep can be done by the kids, though.

While you're cooking, you can give the kids piles of cold cuts and have them make a super-long Italian hero. Or they can have a contest to see who can build the tallest sandwich. The kids can color the labels you use to identify the dinners you're cooking, and they're always game to help pack the food. I've used Dinner Swap recipes to start a fundraiser cookbook for our daycare and schools. If that interests you and the kids are computer-savvy, they can type up the recipes as you prepare them. Or, if they're too young, they can decorate preprinted recipes. Plain lunchboxes or sandwich sacks can be decorated with paint and stickers as well.

The kids can also mix up a batch of coconut cookies for ice cream sandwiches (page 135) while you finish cooking. It's alright if the raw cookies sit for a while on baking trays in the fridge. When you've finished with the ovens, bake the cookies and let them cool a bit before the kids make the ice cream sandwiches. Any leftover cookies go in lunchboxes. Or, make a half-batch of the Polka-Dot Linzertorte dough and have the kids make cookies.

DINNER SWAP RECIPE SUGGESTIONS

- BAKED RIGATONI WITH SAUSAGE, BUTTERNUT SQUASH, AND KALE (PAGE 81)
- FANCY POT ROAST (PAGE 74)
- DUCK AND ANDOUILLE JAMBALAYA (PAGE 72)
- BACON-WRAPPED MEAT LOAF WITH SECRET SPINACH (PAGE 66)
- GRANDMA BEA'S BEEF AND BARLEY SOUP (PAGE 49)

These need to marinate, so just send them home in the marinade and they can be cooked midweek:

- CHINATOWN ROAST PORK (PAGE 71)
- FRIDGE RIBS (PAGE 70)

DESSERT FOR THE PLAYDATE

- COCONUT ICE CREAM SANDWICHES
- POLKA-DOT LINZERTORTE (PAGE 119)

CHAPTER 6 | **SIDES AND SALADS**

Sides and salads inject a bit of personality into the middle of a meal. Think of them as accessories—they give you the chance to take a risk with an accent of stronger flavors or unusual ingredients. They also give you an opportunity to introduce new vegetables to the smaller set. Easy to toss together, sides and salads can make the meal when served alongside a rotisserie chicken, basic roast, or another complicated main dish. Your kids may surprise you, too—vegetables they would never touch get gobbled up when roasted with cheese or tossed with vinaigrette. Pairing a rich side dish with a lean turkey breast or grilled fish is a way to eat healthier without feeling deprived.

GREEK ROASTED POTATOES

These potatoes are crunchy, soaked with a bright lemon flavor, and accented with fresh herbs and bubbling feta cheese. It's a miracle they even make it onto the serving platter, since I greedily steal away the best bits that are stuck in the corners of the sheet pan. And definitely use the largest pan you have so that you get golden goodness and not soft, steamed potatoes. A quarter of the recipe makes the perfect solo supper with a salad—just add a glass of wine and a thick novel.

2 lemons

2 pounds small red, white, or fingerling potatoes, halved

⅓ cup extra-virgin olive oil

5 sprigs fresh oregano, or ½ teaspoon dried, plus extra sprigs for garnish

4 cloves garlic, crushed

1 teaspoon kosher salt

½ pound feta cheese, crumbled

2 cloves garlic, finely chopped (optional)

Freshly ground pepper

○ Preheat the oven to 425 degrees F.

○ Heat a large rimmed baking sheet in the preheated oven. Juice the lemons, and then quarter them. In a large bowl, toss the potatoes, olive oil, oregano, lemon juice, leftover lemon quarters, garlic cloves, and salt.

○ Carefully spread out the potatoes in the heated sheet pan. Roast for 25 to 30 minutes, stirring with a spatula to turn the potatoes occasionally, until the potatoes are almost cooked.

○ Remove from the oven, sprinkle the feta and the chopped garlic on top, if using, and bake for another 8 minutes, until the cheese has become slightly browned and crusty. Season with salt and pepper to taste and garnish with more oregano sprigs.

SERVES 4

NOTE Heating the sheet pan ensures crispier potatoes.

○ **KIDS IN THE KITCHEN** ○

Older kids can halve the potatoes and juice and quarter the lemons. Younger ones can peel the garlic, measure the ingredients, and toss everything together before baking.

DAD'S CAMPFIRE POTATOES

After a long day of fishing on our boat, my dad and I used to cook these foil-wrapped potato bundles long and slow, tucked into the fire alongside whatever my brothers and I caught, or, let's be honest, bought on the way back from the marina. Nowadays I start the potatoes in the microwave, and let them cool a bit before the kids stuff them with bay leaves, thinly sliced onions, and slivers of butter. I then finish them on the grill. In the winter we roast them in the oven until the onions are sweet and caramelized.

4 large russet potatoes, washed

1 tablespoon salt, plus more to taste

½ tablespoon freshly ground pepper, plus more to taste

1 large sweet onion, halved and cut into thin half-moons

16 to 20 bay leaves (see Note)

½ cup (1 stick butter), halved lengthwise and cut crosswise into ¼-inch-thick pieces

Sour cream or crème fraîche for serving

- Poke the potatoes with a fork, about 4 pokes per potato. Place in the micro-wave and cook on high for about 7 to 10 minutes, until almost cooked through (test with the point of a knife). Allow the potatoes to cool slightly. (This can be done a few hours ahead.)

- Meanwhile, prepare a hot grill. Cut 4 large pieces of foil to wrap the potatoes. Place a potato on each square, and cut the potatoes crosswise, three-quarters of the way through, in ½-inch intervals, about 5 cuts. Sprinkle each cavity with salt and pepper. Into each incision, place a half-moon of onion and a piece of the cut butter. Tuck 4 bay leaves into each potato and sprinkle salt and pepper into each incision. Quickly seal the potato with the foil, as the butter may begin to melt if the potatoes are still warm.

- Cook the potatoes for about 20 minutes, until the onions are soft and golden brown. Or preheat the oven to 375 degrees F, and bake for about 25 minutes.

- Serve with sour cream or crème fraîche.

SERVES 4

NOTE If the bay leaves are very large, break them in half. You can also assemble the potato bundles a few hours before; just let the potatoes cool a bit so that the butter doesn't melt.

◦ KIDS IN THE KITCHEN ◦

Younger kids can wash, stuff, and wrap the cooled potatoes. Older kids can slice the potatoes and onions under supervision.

CONFETTI SPAGHETTI

This is an incredibly easy side dish with a huge "wow!" factor. It personifies the rustic yet inventive food my friend Jimmy Bradley serves at his New York City restaurant The Red Cat. This is a variation of a recipe he gave me when I was grumbling over my children's boredom with vegetables. It's practically guaranteed to amuse kids of all ages, and it makes a great partner for grilled or roasted fish, especially swordfish. You can also serve it as a main dish. My daughter Natasha never tires of watching the "spaghetti" magically appear when she runs a fork through the flesh. The nutty flavor of the browned butter and the saltiness of the capers accentuate the sweetness of the squash.

1 large spaghetti squash

2 tablespoons extra virgin olive oil

¼ teaspoon kosher salt

⅛ teaspoon freshly ground pepper

6 tablespoons sweet butter

2 tablespoons capers, drained

1 zucchini, seeded and diced (see Note)

1 red bell pepper, seeded, deribbed, and diced

¼ cup fresh lemon juice

¼ cup chopped fresh parsley

Coarse salt and freshly ground pepper

1 small tomato, seeded and chopped

Freshly grated Parmigiano-Reggiano

○ Preheat the oven to 400 degrees F.

○ Cut the squash in half lengthwise and scoop out all the seeds. Rub the squash inside and out with the oil and season the inside with salt and pepper. Place the squash, cut side down, on a baking sheet and cover with foil. Bake for 45 minutes, or until the rind is slightly soft and gives with a little pressure. With a fork, scrape out the flesh into an ovenproof bowl, creating the thin strands of "spaghetti." Cover and keep warm in a very low oven. This can be done ahead of time and rewarmed in a low oven or microwave.

○ Heat a large sauté pan over medium-high heat, and melt the butter. Brown the butter carefully until it turns dark brown in color, but is not burned. Add the capers, zucchini, and red bell pepper and stir quickly to stop the butter from cooking any further. Remove from the heat when warmed through. Add the lemon juice, parsley, salt, and pepper.

○ In a large serving bowl or platter, mix the squash, butter-sauce mixture, and diced tomato. Sprinkle with cheese and serve immediately.

SERVES 4

NOTE To remove the seeds from the zucchini, cut off both ends and cut crosswise in half. Stand the zucchini on one end and carefully cut down one side of the core, as if you were coring an apple. Turn and continue until the seeded core remains. Discard the core, and continue to dice the green slices of zucchini.

○ **KIDS IN THE KITCHEN** ○

You can cook the squash ahead, pre-chop the veggies, and have the kids play magician with the squash as you brown the butter while everyone's at the table. Younger kids can help scoop out seeds from the raw squash, rub the cut squash with oil and seasonings, and magically (and carefully if squash is hot) create spaghetti strands with a fork. Older kids can chop the vegetables while supervised.

BROWN BUTTER

Browning butter adds a lovely nutty flavor, but it can take a few tries if you've never done it before. If you're using a dark pan it's a good idea to have a white or cream plate on which to test a drop of the butter, so you can see the color. You can also lower the level of the heat, but it will take a little longer to get that desired rich brown color. Here's where the type of butter you choose can make a difference. An imported or premium butter, like Plugra, has less sediment, which tends to burn faster.

Brown butter dresses up plain steamed vegetables. Add a few handfuls of slivered, blanched almonds when you start the butter, and they will toast along with the butter. When the butter and almonds are done, add a squeeze of lemon, season with salt and pepper, and toss with steamed string beans, or asparagus.

TANGLED GREEN SALAD WITH LEMON PITA

This dish, which ends up looking like a bed of overgrown ivy, was inspired by a Persian salad that a friend's mother showed me many years ago. The tangled greens make a perfect bed for grilled chicken or fish. Let the kids customize their salad blend. Consider buying some of the herbs in pots instead of bunches, so the kids can grow them in a garden or window box. In the winter you can use a cast-iron skillet instead of the outdoor grill for the pitas; just make sure you press down firmly with a spatula to ensure crispness.

FOR THE SALAD

2 bunches watercress, washed of sand and bottom stems trimmed

1 bunch scallions, thinly sliced

1 small bunch dill leaves, coarsely chopped, or torn whole sprigs

⅓ cup fresh mint, coarsely chopped or torn

⅓ cup fresh basil leaves, coarsely chopped or torn

¼ cup fresh cilantro leaves, coarsely chopped or whole

FOR THE DRESSING

½ cup plain yogurt

Zest and juice of ½ lemon

½ teaspoon champagne vinegar

⅛ cup olive oil

¼ teaspoon salt

⅛ teaspoon freshly ground pepper

FOR THE PITA

2 large pita breads

¼ cup olive oil

1 lemon, halved

Salt and freshly ground pepper

½ teaspoon ground cumin (optional)

○ In a large bowl, toss all of the salad ingredients. Or if you want to top with grilled meat or fish, layer the watercress on a platter and scatter the herbs evenly on top. Set aside.

○ In a small bowl whisk together all of the dressing ingredients and set aside.

○ Prepare a hot grill or preheat a cast-iron skillet or grill pan over high heat. To make the pitas, brush the oil over both sides. Squeeze the lemon over both sides of the pitas, and season well with salt and pepper. Sprinkle with cumin if using. Grill for about 1 to 2 minutes per side, pressing down with a spatula, until very well toasted but still slightly soft inside. Remove from the grill or pan and cut into quarters.

○ Drizzle the dressing over the salad. Tuck wedges of pita along the sides and serve immediately.

SERVES 4

NOTE If you're pressed for time, skip the dressing and toss the greens with lemon and extra-virgin olive oil.

○ KIDS IN THE KITCHEN ○

Kids of most ages can help wash and dry the watercress and herbs, tear herbs, season the pitas, make the dressing, and arrange the salad.

SWEET POTATO SALAD WITH LIME AND ANCHO

I first came up with this sweet-and-sour and subtly spicy salad as a side dish for Mathias's annual birthday Burger Bar bash, served along-side the Spicy Slaw (facing page) and all the toppings on page 68. I like to hold back a third of the potatoes to mix without the chili powder so the kids and heat-averse adults can have a slightly milder version. Take care not to overcook the sweet potatoes so they hold their shape when you toss them with the dressing. A shower of roasted pumpkin seeds added at the end give the dish a nice bit of crunch.

4 pounds (about 6 potatoes) sweet potatoes, peeled and cut into 2-inch chunks

1 cup chopped scallions (about 1 bunch)

¼ teaspoon freshly ground pepper

1 teaspoon kosher salt, plus more for seasoning

Zest and juice of 3 limes

½ cup fruity olive oil

1 teaspoon honey

½ teaspoon ancho chile powder

Roasted pumpkin seeds for garnish (optional)

○ Put the potatoes in a large saucepan filled with cold water over high heat and bring to a boil. Reduce to medium-high heat and cook until a knife easily pierces the flesh, about 10 to 13 minutes. Do not overcook the potatoes; they should be firm, but slightly tender.

○ Meanwhile, in a large bowl, whisk together the remaining ingredients, except for the pumpkin seeds. Set aside. Drain the potatoes and sprinkle them with a generous pinch of salt. Add the warm potatoes to the dressing and toss them gently with a large spatula. Serve at room temperature or slightly chilled, garnished with the pumpkin seeds, if desired.

SERVES 6

○ KIDS IN THE KITCHEN ○

Older kids can peel potatoes, cut the potatoes and scallions, and also learn how to test the potatoes for doneness while being supervised. Younger kids can measure the ingredients and mix the dressing, carefully toss salad, garnish, and serve.

SPICY SLAW

After Anthony developed an allergy to shellfish a few years ago, summers weren't the same. So I devised this coleslaw with crab seasoning as an homage to the crab-cracking days of summer. Now he can still have that right-off-the-docks experience while he eats his steamed knockwurst, rather than steamed crabs! He likes it fairly spicy, so I pass the hot sauce to make sure the kids don't scream.

1 head green cabbage

1 cup mayonnaise

1 tablespoon crab seasoning, preferably Old Bay brand

1 tablespoon sugar

½ teaspoon kosher salt, plus more to taste

¼ teaspoon freshly ground pepper

2 teaspoons celery seeds

1 tablespoon Dijon mustard

1½ tablespoons cider vinegar

○ Cut the cabbage in half and remove the core. Cut by hand into shreds, or cut into wedges, and stack the wedges in the wide feed tube of the food processor, and shred with the shredding disc. Set aside.

○ In a large bowl, combine the mayonnaise, crab seasoning, sugar, salt and pepper, celery seeds, mustard, and vinegar. Combine the cabbage with the mixture, making sure it's evenly coated. This is easiest to do with your hands—and lots of fun for the kids. The coleslaw is best made a few hours in advance so the flavors can blend. Add salt to taste. Keep refrigerated.

SERVES 6

NOTE You can substitute a bag of pre-cut coleslaw mix for the cabbage.

○ **KIDS IN THE KITCHEN** ○

Much older kids can try to cut the cabbage under supervision, and help with the food processor, if being used. Kids of almost any age can help measure the ingredients and mix with their hands.

ASIAN RADICCHIO SLAW

It's rare to see radicchio cut like cabbage, into ribbons, and even more rare to see it with an Asian accent. This is one of the fastest sides around, so I tend to keep a head of radicchio in the veggie bin, as it keeps well, too. The seasoned rice vinegar lends a sweet contrast to the bitter radicchio. It's excellent paired with something slightly sweet, like the Sticky Wings (page 54) or Chinatown Roast Pork (page 71). Or use it to dress up a store-bought roast chicken, grilled shrimp, or, even better, a duck from a Chinese takeout restaurant. This presentation works well when dressed with the more traditional balsamic dressing, too.

2 heads radicchio

2 teaspoons toasted sesame oil

3 teaspoons seasoned rice vinegar

Juice of 1 orange

1½ teaspoons sugar

Salt and freshly ground pepper

○ Remove any tired or brown outer leaves from the radicchio. Cut each head in half and remove the white core from each half. Place cut side down and cut the radicchio into thin ribbons, as if you were cutting cabbage for coleslaw.

○ Put in a large bowl, sprinkle with the sesame oil, toss, and sprinkle with the vinegar, orange juice, sugar, salt and pepper to taste, and toss again. Transfer to a serving bowl for a side dish. Or spread it on a platter to make a bed, and top with duck, or whatever you like.

SERVES 4 TO 6

NOTE You can cut the radicchio into ribbons a day in advance; wrap the cut-up radicchio in paper towel, place in a sealed plastic bag, and refrigerate.

○ **KIDS IN THE KITCHEN** ○

Older kids can cut the radicchio into ribbons under supervision. Younger ones can juice the orange, measure the ingredients, toss, and make the bed.

BRUSSELS SPROUTS WITH BACON AND CREAM

I have been unable to vary our Thanksgiving meal for the past five years. Every time I try, one family member or another cries that I've left out the one thing they cherish about the holiday. My brother Jeffrey would stop speaking to me if I left these off the menu, and since we usually hold the dinner at his house, I'm happy to oblige. If you're lucky enough to see Brussels sprouts on the stalk, buy them. The stalk is easily one of the most interesting-looking vegetables out there, and may help some of your guests overcome their sprout phobia.

5 cups Brussels sprouts (1 large stalk)

¼ pound bacon, cut crosswise into ¼-inch pieces

½ cup heavy cream

½ to 1 teaspoon salt (depending on saltiness of bacon)

½ teaspoon freshly ground pepper

SPECIAL EQUIPMENT: large metal colander (see Notes)

○ If the sprouts are on the stalk, remove them with a small paring knife and rinse carefully. Remove any thickness at the base, and halve the sprouts. Fill a large Dutch oven or saucepan with a few inches of water. Put the metal steamer in the pot and bring to a boil. Add the Brussels sprouts, and when the water is boiling, cover and steam for 5 minutes or until tender and a knife can easily pierce the center of a Brussels sprout. Check the water level midway through steaming and add additional water if needed. Remove from the steamer and set aside. This can be done a day in advance, as they are rewarmed in the sauce.

○ In the same Dutch oven, over medium-high heat, sauté the bacon until crisp. Set aside, drain and discard the fat, and return the bacon to the pan. Add the steamed Brussels sprouts and heavy cream and simmer until the cream is thick and reduced, about 6 to 10 minutes. Season with the salt and pepper.

SERVES 6 TO 8

NOTES Steaming the Brussels sprouts keeps the colors nice and bright. I usually cook up an extra cup of sprouts to toss with lemon, olive oil, and chopped fresh thyme for the vegetarians (or more health-conscious) at the table.

5 cups is a large quantity, so, rather than steaming in batches, try fitting a large metal colander in your biggest pot. If the handles peek out, cover with foil, but do not let the foil touch the sprouts.

○ **KIDS IN THE KITCHEN** ○

Older kids can remove the sprouts from the stalk if using and halve them. Younger kids can help prepare the steamer basket away from the heat, and measure the ingredients.

HOLIDAY MENUS

I think a well-choreographed potluck is the best way to have a relaxed, yet delicious holiday meal. Make what you love to do and would really miss on the table, and assign the rest of the meal to family and friends, or order it from local specialty take-out shops. If baking's not your thing, buy the pies and cakes, or beg your mother-in-law to make her specialty. Use the freezer and get a head start. The point is to not be exhausted, and to enjoy yourself with your family and friends.

Here are a few menu suggestions for a few holidays.

THANKSGIVING

- PICKLED SHRIMP WITH MANGO AND FENNEL (PAGE 47)
- ROAST TURKEY
- SESAME ORZO WITH DRIED APRICOT, CURRANTS, AND SLIVERED ALMONDS (PAGE 111)
- BRUSSELS SPROUTS WITH BACON AND CREAM (PAGE 100)
- CURRIED ROASTED CAULIFLOWER (PAGE 103)
- POLKA-DOT LINZERTORTE (PAGE 119)

HANUKKAH

- STUFFED DATES (PAGE 36)
- POTATO PANCAKES WITH BACON AND CHEESE (TRY WITH SWEET POTATOES, AND SKIP THE BACON!) (PAGE 168)
- FANCY POT ROAST (PAGE 74)
- CHOCOLATE CHERRY CHUNK CAKE (PAGE 122)
- RUGGIES (AUNT LINDA'S RUGALACH) (PAGE 132)

CHRISTMAS

- NO-FRY CANDIED SPICED PECANS (PAGE 33)
- PARMESAN SHORTBREAD (PAGE 53)
- DUCK AND ANDOUILLE JAMBALAYA (PAGE 72)
- MERINGUE CLOUD (VARIATION OF MERINGUE SNOWBALLS, PAGE 139)
- STICKY TOFFEE PUDDING (PAGE 140)

EASTER

- 1-2-3 CHEESE TART (PAGE 39)
- MINT TEA ROAST LAMB (PAGE 59)
- GREEK ROASTED POTATOES (PAGE 89)
- TANGLED GREEN SALAD WITH LEMON PITA (PAGE 95)
- LAUREN'S LEMON SQUARES (PAGE 125)
- PANNA COTTA WITH BALSAMIC STRAWBERRIES AND PEPPER (PAGE 144)
- HONEY AND LIME FRUIT SALAD (PAGE 121)

CURRIED ROASTED CAULIFLOWER

Roast cauliflower at high heat, and it becomes a completely different vegetable. The sugars caramelize, the flavor deepens, and the cauliflower takes on a lovely nutty character. Prepared this way, I've surprised many parents as their kids clamor for more. It's great roasted with just olive oil, but toss in a few spices and it really stands out as an ideal complement for lamb chops, pork roast, or the everyday roast chicken.

Sometimes I make my own spice mixture when I have the time, but more often I just reach for store-bought Madras curry powder or garam masala. You can use yellow mustard seeds, but try to find the black ones that show up all the time in Indian cooking. They're really worth seeking out, for the distinctive aroma and crunch they add to this dish. When we were living in Los Angeles, I once bought 5 pounds of brown mustard seeds at an Indian restaurant supply store. Anthony thought I was nuts, but the color is so beautiful, I kept them displayed in a big glass jar. They're inexpensive, and you can find places to order them in the Sources (page 173).

1 head cauliflower, cut into small florets

⅓ cup extra virgin olive oil

½ teaspoon salt

⅛ teaspoon freshly ground pepper

1 tablespoon Madras curry powder or garam masala

1 tablespoon black or yellow mustard seeds

○ Preheat the oven to 425 degrees F.

○ Toss all the ingredients in a bowl and spread evenly on a rimmed baking sheet or in a large roasting pan. Try not to crowd the cauliflower; otherwise, it will steam and you won't get the delicious caramelized bits. Roast for 20 to 25 minutes, shaking the pan and stirring the cauliflower midway through roasting.

○ Transfer to a serving dish and taste for seasoning; you may need another sprinkling of salt and a grinding of fresh pepper.

SERVES 4

○ **KIDS IN THE KITCHEN** ○

Older kids can separate the cauliflower into florets with a small knife, under supervision, and younger ones can help with their hands or a plastic knife, and measure and mix the ingredients together.

BALSAMIC CHERRY TOMATO SALAD

Finding good tomatoes year-round is tricky, so I often rely on cherry tomatoes. There are many different varieties available lately, from the super Sweet 100s to the pear and golden yellows. A pinch of sugar helps a bit, too. Serve over the Parmesan Chicken Fingers (page 83) for an addictive main course.

2 pints cherry tomatoes, halved

2 tablespoons balsamic vinegar

3 to 4 tablespoons extra virgin olive oil

Pinch of sugar

¼ teaspoon salt

⅛ teaspoon freshly ground pepper

¼ cup basil leaves, cut into thin ribbons

½ pound baby arugula or watercress

Place the tomatoes in a large bowl, add the remaining ingredients, and combine gently with a spatula or wooden spoon. Serve over a bed of arugula or watercress.

SERVES 4

○ KIDS IN THE KITCHEN ○

Here's the chance for some teamwork; younger kids can stack and roll the basil leaves, and the older ones can cut them under supervision. Most kids can measure the ingredients and mix and serve the salad.

SNOW WHITE'S SALAD

I created this salad in honor of Natasha's current favorite fairy tale. The pomegranate adds a ghoulish touch for Mathias, who loves all things scary. A silver oval platter which resembles the evil queen's mirror makes a spooky serving plate. The salad was also a way to introduce the kids to different lettuces. It actually prompted a great discussion about color that inspired me to create a week of monochromatic dinners. Each night's dinner was centered around a color they selected. The kids loved this idea—with the possible exception of the veggie-heavy "green night."

FOR THE VINAIGRETTE

2 teaspoons honey

2 tablespoons balsamic vinegar

1 teaspoon fresh lemon juice

½ teaspoon kosher salt

⅛ teaspoon freshly ground pepper

⅓ cup olive oil

1 tablespoon fresh tarragon or chervil, finely chopped

FOR THE SALAD

1 head frisée (French chicory)

2 fennel bulbs, halved, cored, and cut into thin slices

2 to 3 heads endive, cut crosswise into ½-inch rings

⅓ cup blue cheese, crumbled (preferably Maytag Blue)

1 pomegranate, quartered and seeded (see Note)

○ In a small bowl, whisk all of the vinaigrette ingredients together and set aside.

○ To make the salad, in a large, shallow serving bowl or platter, arrange a bed of frisée. Top with the fennel and endive. Scatter the cheese. Sprinkle with the pomegranate seeds. Drizzle with the vinaigrette right before serving.

SERVES 6

NOTE Seed the pomegranate over a bowl or on a small board in the sink, as the juice will stain. You can also sprinkle the seeds over fruit salads.

◦ KIDS IN THE KITCHEN ◦

Most kids can help wash and dry the salad greens, crumble cheese, seed the pomegranate (while wearing clothes you won't mind getting stained), measure the ingredients, whisk the vinaigrette, and arrange and dress the salad on the platter. Older kids can cut the lettuce under supervision.

TOMATO-COCONUT SALSA

Tomatoes, onions, cilantro…but wait! With a shower of coconut and cumin seeds and a sprinkling of chili powder, this Indian version pushes away any memories of the same old salsa for grilled fish (sea bass, snapper, tuna, or salmon), chicken, or even lamb. I eat this straight from the bowl or with toasted naan or pita bread. It's the kind of dish that you can easily throw together quickly. Make half a batch without the chiles if the kids don't do spicy.

2 pints cherry tomatoes, halved

1 cucumber, peeled and cut into medium dice or thin half-moons

1 small onion, thinly sliced into half-moons

½ cup chopped fresh cilantro

4 tablespoons shredded unsweetened coconut (see Notes)

1 teaspoon cumin seeds

1 to 2 serrano chiles, chopped, or ½ teaspoon chili powder

Juice of 1 lime or lemon

½ teaspoon salt

○ Toss all the ingredients together gently in a large bowl, and taste for seasoning. Add additional salt or chili powder to taste.

SERVES 4 TO 6

NOTES The unsweetened coconut will probably require a trip to the health food store. You don't want to use the sweetened coconut from the baking aisle. I promise it will be worth the extra trip. Experiment with the finely shredded or large shards of coconut, too.

Gently toast the cumin seeds for about 30 seconds in a dry pan to deepen the flavor.

○ **KIDS IN THE KITCHEN** ○

Older kids can help slice the vegetables under supervision. Younger ones can help measure, juice the citrus, and toss the ingredients.

BROCCOLI RABE

I make a batch of these classically Italian bitter greens almost every week, and find that the splash of chicken stock adds a mild sweetness and tempers the bite. Simmering them in a large pan is simpler than blanching and sautéing, which is the usual method. Broccoli rabe is perfect alongside a plate of grilled sausages and they're also a nice accompaniment to the 300-Degree Pork Roast (page 67). My kids like it best when tossed along with a handful of currants and toasted pine nuts into some farfalle pasta.

2 pounds broccoli rabe (about 2 bunches)

¼ cup olive oil

4 cloves garlic, peeled and lightly crushed

½ cup chicken stock

½ teaspoon salt

¼ teaspoon freshly ground pepper

1 lemon, quartered

○ Rinse any grit from the broccoli rabe, but do not dry. Spread the broccoli on the cutting board and, with a large knife, trim off the bottom inch of the stalks and discard. Cut across the stalks again, midway between the top of the florets and the bottom of the stalks. Keep the stalks separate from the florets and set aside.

○ Heat the oil in a large sauté pan over medium-high heat and add the garlic cloves and broccoli stalks. Cover the pan and cook for 3 minutes, stirring occasionally. Add the florets and the chicken stock and continue cooking for 3 to 5 minutes, stirring occasionally until the broccoli rabe is tender. Season with the salt and pepper and serve with lemon wedges.

SERVES 4

VARIATION Add a drizzle of slightly bitter Tuscan extra-virgin olive oil to accentuate the flavor; coarsely chop and serve piled on garlic toast.

○ **KIDS IN THE KITCHEN** ○

Kids can help wash the greens, peel the garlic, measure the ingredients, and garnish with the lemon wedges. Older kids can help cut the broccoli rabe under supervision.

WINTER WHITE MENU

There's something zany yet sophisticated about trying to have an all-white meal, and I confess I'm nerdy and make everyone wear white. All shades count, ecru, cream, and pale almond. For a fun project I pick up the paper rectangular white paint samples from the hardware store, and make collages for place cards. One adult friend made white elephant collages for the kids to take home.

- WHITE CRUDITÉ: white radishes, fennel, and jicama, served with goat cheese, thinned with a little heavy cream and mixed with herbs

- SNOW WHITE'S SALAD (PAGE 105)

- 300-DEGREE PORK ROAST (PAGE 67)

- MASHED POTATOES

- MERINGUE SNOWBALLS OR CLOUD (PAGE 138), OR COCONUT TARTLETS WITH WHIPPED CREAM AND WHITE RASPBERRIES, OR STORE-BOUGHT VANILLA OR DULCE DE LECHE ICE CREAM

SESAME ORZO WITH DRIED APRICOTS, CURRANTS, AND SLIVERED ALMONDS

Orzo, a type of pasta that is often overlooked, is a pantry staple in our house. I toss it into soups when they are too thin, or with butter and Parmesan and scallions for a twist on mac and cheese. Its slippery texture works well for cold pasta salad, like this fragrant fruit-studded version. It is my take on a cult recipe from the beloved *Frog Commissary Cookbook*, which we used at a catering company years ago. If your kids aren't fans of cilantro, switch to chopped parsley or mint. Serve this with duck, grilled shrimp, steak, store-bought roast chicken, or as a main-course salad.

1 pound orzo pasta

¼ cup toasted sesame oil

½ cup canola or vegetable oil

½ cup rice vinegar or cider vinegar

Zest of 1 orange, plus 2 tablespoons of the juice

2 teaspoons soy sauce

2 teaspoons sugar, or 1 tablespoon honey

2 teaspoons kosher salt

½ teaspoon freshly ground pepper

One 2-inch piece ginger, peeled and grated

1 large clove garlic, finely chopped

2 scallions, thinly sliced, plus 1 for garnish

¾ cup fresh cilantro, chopped

1 cup slivered almonds, toasted (see Notes)

⅔ cup diced dried apricots (see Notes)

½ cup currants

◎ Cook the pasta according to package directions, until *al dente,* or firm to the bite. Drain, but do not rinse.

◎ In a large bowl, whisk together the oils, vinegar, orange zest and juice, soy sauce, sugar, salt, pepper, ginger, and garlic, and set aside. Mix the pasta and dressing together and stir in the remaining ingredients. The salad can be served warm or chilled. If serving chilled, recheck the seasoning when you are ready to serve. Garnish with reserved scallions.

SERVES 6 TO 8

NOTES To toast the almonds, preheat the oven to 375 degrees F. Spread the nuts on a baking sheet and place on the middle oven rack. Toast for about 6 minutes, shaking the pan occasionally, until the nuts are golden and fragrant. Immediately remove from hot pan so they do not continue to cook.

Lightly oil the knife blade before dicing the apricots so they don't stick to the knife.

◦ **KIDS IN THE KITCHEN** ◦

Older kids can help test the pasta for doneness under supervision (you can rinse the pasta to cool it). Most kids can help zest the orange and grate the ginger, measure the ingredients, mix the vinaigrette, and serve.

○ SALAD BAR PLAYDATE ○

Whether you have a wonderful plot of dirt for the kids to plant or live in a skyscraper apartment, this playdate can be easily adapted so the kids can get their hands dirty. It came out of a project about healthful foods that I designed for my son's science class. Of course, when you mention vegetables, everyone groans and runs. The trick is to get them engaged and challenged. First they plant individual "salad bars" in window boxes. Then they make salad dressings to take home, and crudités sculptures and dips to enjoy at the playdate.

For the window boxes you can either find kits at the hardware store, or buy potting soil, window boxes, and salad seeds, and let the kids pick their seeds. Mix in some heirloom seeds, edible flowers, and unusual herbs so that everyone has to try at least one new thing in his or her box. Pick up an extra-large roll of cellophane paper to wrap the planted window boxes like big bouquets for easy transport. Print up care and watering directions on little cards, or tie the seed cards to the "bouquet."

For the salad dressings, prepare canning jars or, better yet, plastic squeeze bottles. Have markers and stickers to make labels. The kids can toss the dressing with a salad they help the parents make at home while the salad bar grows.

Next let the kids make their own crudités sculptures with toothpicks and skewers. Then they can invent their own dips. For the crudités, buy both regular-size veggies for the older kids to cut up, and baby-size veggies for younger kids. I always throw in a mystery veggie like a jicama and have them taste it blindfolded. Set out trays with yogurt, low-fat sour cream, hummus, spices, and herbs for making their own dips.

MENU (try any combination of these recipes)

- 1-2-3 CHEESE TART (PAGE 39)
- SLOW-COOKED SALMON WITH SALSA VERDE (PAGE 65)
- GRILLED FISH WITH TOMATO-COCONUT SALSA (PAGE 107)
- ARUGULA-ALMOND PESTO WITH PASTA AND GRILLED SHRIMP (PAGE 77)
- 300-DEGREE PORK ROAST (PAGE 67)
- MINT TEA ROAST LAMB (PAGE 59)
- CONFETTI SPAGHETTI (PAGE 92)
- ASIAN RADICCHIO SLAW (PAGE 99)
- TANGLED GREEN SALAD WITH LEMON PITA (PAGE 95)
- SNOW WHITE'S SALAD (PAGE 105)
- HONEY AND LIME FRUIT SALAD (PAGE 121)
- CHOCOLATE TOASTED ALMOND ICE CREAM (a reward for eating all those veggies, PAGE 137)

LIGHTEN UP MENU

Whether it's after the winter holidays, or just the right time, here are recipes that have big and bold flavors without the fat and calories. Start with a Bananaberry Smoothie (page 167) in the morning.

MENU

- EDAMAME DIP (PAGE 41)
- PARCHMENT-BAKED HALIBUT WITH SHIITAKES, LEMONS, AND HERBS (PAGE 61)
- TANGLED GREEN SALAD WITH LEMON PITA (PAGE 95)
- HONEY AND LIME FRUIT SALAD (PAGE 121)

CHAPTER 7 | **SWEETS**

Bribery for eating vegetables? Just a minor reason to whip up a dessert. Most kids love to bake: The danger level is relatively low, and the mad scientist experience is fairly high. These recipes are pretty forgiving and just beg for an extra pair (or two) of helping hands. Most can be made far in advance. They're practical, too. If a recipe calls for a bunch of egg whites, such as the Brown Sugar Angel Food Cake (page 130), there's a recipe for using up the yolks nearby (Lime Curd, page 131). There are suggested variations that you can divvy up between the kids to push their creative thinking; meringues take on many flavors and forms (page 138). Also, baking or decorating projects are a good way to end a playdate or birthday party, because then your friends can go home with their sweet handiwork.

LEMON POLENTA CAKE

I had run out of olive oil when I went to bake this Italian style cake for the school bake sale. Of course it was late at night and the kids were sleeping, so there was no way I was making it to the grocery store. I tinkered a bit and substituted butter for the olive oil. Amazingly enough, it was so good that it sold out the next morning.

I've made this with fancy Italian polenta and supermarket cornmeal. Either is fine, just don't use a coarsely ground cornmeal because the texture is too pronounced. You can also substitute white sugar for the brown in a pinch. The kids like this cake for an afternoon snack, but it can be dressed up easily with mounds of raspberries and whipped cream for dessert. It keeps well for days, too.

FOR THE CAKE

¾ cup (1½ sticks) unsalted butter, at room temperature, cut into pieces

1¼ cups light brown sugar

4 eggs

Zest and juice of 3 lemons

¾ cup polenta or yellow cornmeal

¾ cup self-rising cake flour (see Note)

FOR THE GLAZE

¾ cup confectioners' sugar

2 to 3 tablespoons milk or water

FOR THE GARNISH

Thin lemon slices

1 pint raspberries

○ Preheat the oven to 350 degrees F. Butter the inside of one 8-inch cake pan and line the bottom with parchment or waxed paper. Butter the paper, then dust the entire pan with flour. Tap out the excess and set aside.

○ To make the cake, in the bowl of a stand mixer, beat the butter on medium-high speed until light and fluffy. Slowly beat in the brown sugar and continue beating until the mixture is creamy and smooth, about 2 minutes. Beat in the eggs, one at a time, fully incorporating each one before adding the next. Add the lemon zest and juice. The mixture may look messy, but that is fine.

○ In a medium bowl, whisk the polenta and flour together. Add the dry mixture to the batter, 1 cup at a time, mixing on low speed. Pour and spread out the batter in the cake pan, and gently tap to remove any air bubbles.

○ Bake until a toothpick inserted in the center comes out clean, about 35 to 40 minutes, turning the pan midway through baking.

○ Allow the cake to cool in the pan for about 10 minutes. Invert onto a cooling rack, and carefully turn the cake right side up. To make the glaze, mix the confectioners' sugar with the milk and drizzle over the cake while still warm. Garnish with lemon slices and raspberries, and serve warm or at room temperature with whipped cream.

SERVES 6 TO 8

NOTE If you don't have self-rising cake flour, combine 1⅛ teaspoons of baking powder and ⅜ teaspoon of salt with ¾ cup of all-purpose flour.

○ **KIDS IN THE KITCHEN** ○

Most kids can help prepare the pan; cut the softened butter with a plastic knife, under supervision; and help measure the dry ingredients. They can also juice the lemons and whisk the flour and polenta. They can help mix the glaze, pour it over the cake, and garnish the top. Older kids can zest the lemons, too.

POLKA-DOT LINZERTORTE

This torte is the perfect example of a recipe that has evolved through my life as a working mother. I used to make a fancy lattice top for it that drove me crazy—rolling the dough, chilling the dough, weaving it—ugh! I would only brave this recipe once a year for my cousin Barry Sonnenfeld's birthday, dragging it to the set of whatever movie he was currently directing. A true labor of love, emphasis on labor.

I finally realized I could simply press the dough into the pan, instead of rolling and transferring a slippery 14-inch Frisbee. Then I gave the torte a more chic, modern look by replacing the traditional lattice top with round cutouts in different sizes, just like the cookies the kids and I would make with the leftover dough. My newer, sleeker polka-dot torte reminded me of a mod Jonathan Adler vase. Things were now very cool—both my groovy new torte and my temper. This is an enormous torte, which will keep for a week. The kids clamor for it at breakfast.

4½ cups walnuts (about 1 pound)

3 cups all-purpose flour

¼ teaspoon salt

1¼ cups sugar

2 teaspoons ground cinnamon

1¼ cups (2½ sticks) cold unsalted butter, cut into small pieces

2 eggs, lightly beaten

2 tablespoons grated lemon or orange zest

1 tablespoon unseasoned breadcrumbs or graham cracker crumbs (about 2 finely crushed crackers)

2 cups seedless raspberry or apricot jam

FOR THE YOLK GLAZE

1 egg yolk

2 teaspoons water

SPECIAL EQUIPMENT: one 12-inch fluted tart pan with removable bottom; circular cookie cutters, ranging from ½ inch to 4 inches in diameter

- Preheat the oven to 400 degrees F.

- In the bowl of a food processor, combine the walnuts and 3 tablespoons of the flour. Pulse to a medium-fine grind, not too fine. Transfer to a large bowl and set aside.

- Combine the remaining flour, the salt, sugar, cinnamon, and butter in the bowl of a food processor, and pulse until the mixture resembles coarse crumbs. Add this mixture to the walnuts and lightly mix the dough with a wooden spoon or your hands. Stir in the eggs and zest and gently press the dough into a disc.

- Set aside one-quarter of the dough for the top. Press the remaining dough into the pan, taking care to make the sides of the tart no more than ¼ inch thick because the crusts get very firm when baked.

- Place the tart pan on a flat baking sheet and bake for 15 minutes.

- While the tart bottom is baking, gently roll out the remaining dough on a lightly floured surface, using a lightly floured rolling pin, to a thickness of ¼ inch. Using a variety of round cookie cutters in different sizes, cut out polka dots, about 12 to 15 circles, depending on their size. If the dough becomes soft, transfer the circles to wax or parchment paper, and chill them to make handling easier. Set the leftover dough aside to use for cookies (see Notes) or discard.

- Remove the tart pan from the oven and set on a cooling rack.

➡ CONTINUED

➡ **CONTINUED**

○ Lower the oven temperature to 350 degrees F. Lightly sprinkle the bread-crumbs or graham cracker crumbs over the bottom of the tart shell. This prevents the crust from becoming too soggy, and keeps the jam from sliding around. Spread the jam evenly over the tart crust. Top the jam with polka dots in a random pattern, leaving about 2 inches of jam showing between the dots.

○ To make the glaze, mix the yolk and water, and lightly brush each polka dot and the top of the tart shell. Return the tart to the oven and bake for 1 hour. The polka dots and the tart shell will be a rich golden brown and the polka dots will be completely baked. Cool completely in the pan on a cooling rack. Carefully remove the outer ring of the tart pan. Serve with ice cream, whipped cream, or crème fraîche, if desired.

SERVES 10 TO 12

NOTES If you don't have a 12-inch tart pan, you can press the dough into a smaller size tart pan, and use the remaining dough to make cookies (see below). Just remember to reduce the final baking time. An 8-inch tart pan will take about 30 to 35 minutes, a 9-inch tart will take about 35 to 40 minutes, and a 10-inch, about 40 to 45 minutes.

If there is extra dough, roll it into logs and cut into cookies. Decorate with colored sugars or edible decorations, and bake at 375 degrees F for 10 to 12 minutes. Or keep them plain, bake, and sandwich with jam. For thumbprint cookies, pinch off and roll into balls, indent with your thumb, fill with jam, and bake as above. The dough can also be frozen for a future cookie-making date.

⊙ KIDS IN THE KITCHEN ⊙

Most kids cans can help measure the ingredients, pulse the food processor (under supervision), mix the dough, and press it into the pan. They can also help roll the dough, punch out the polka dots with the cookie cutters, crack the eggs, and make the glaze. Older kids can paint the glaze on the polka dots, taking care not to touch the hot tart pan.

HONEY AND LIME FRUIT SALAD

When there is ripe fruit growing in your backyard or on display at the farm stand, it usually doesn't need much more than a beautiful bowl or platter to reach its delicious potential. But when the flavors and sweetness need a little coaxing, I find a touch of honey and a squeeze of lime do wonders. Warming the honey in the microwave removes any crystals and helps blend the flavors.

1 honeydew, seeded and cut into large chunks

1 mango, sliced or cut into medium chunks

½ pint raspberries

1 pint strawberries, hulled and halved (or quartered if large)

1 pineapple, cubed

⅓ cup honey

Zest and juice of 1 lime

2 tablespoons fresh mint leaves, cut into thin ribbons

Arrange the fruit on a platter or gently toss together in a large bowl. Put the honey in a microwave-safe measuring cup or bowl, and microwave on high for 15 seconds. Stir in the lime zest and juice and scatter the mint leaves over the top. Drizzle over the platter, or toss with the fruit if serving in a bowl. Serve immediately, or chill until you're ready to serve.

SERVES 6 TO 8

NOTE For a refreshing change, substitute basil for the mint. Or try a flavored honey such as lavender or a rich chestnut. Use a bit less so they don't overwhelm the fruit, and omit the mint.

⊙ KIDS IN THE KITCHEN ⊙

Older kids can trim and cut the fruit under supervision. Younger kids can cut fruit into smaller pieces with a plastic knife, then carefully toss the fruit with the mint, lime, and honey, once it has cooled slightly.

CHOCOLATE CHERRY CHUNK CAKE

Ah, indulgence! Now's the time to break out the Valrhona cocoa powder. This cake is very impressive but oh-so-simple and easy to customize. Play with the flavorings—try white chocolate chunks instead of bittersweet ones. Or add almonds. You can serve this plain, but it really shines when split and frosted with the Sour Cream Ganache (page 124).

The cake keeps well for days. Since the eggs don't need to be separated, and the whites aren't whipped, many children can make this pretty much by themselves.

¾ cup (1½ sticks) unsalted butter at room temperature, plus extra for the pan

1 cup unsweetened cocoa powder, plus extra for the pan

¾ cup all-purpose flour

½ teaspoon baking powder

¼ teaspoon salt

1 cup sugar

3 large eggs

1 teaspoon vanilla extract

⅔ cup sour cream

½ cup bittersweet chocolate chunks

½ cup dried cherries

Sour Cream Ganache (page 124)

○ Preheat the oven to 350 degrees F. Butter the inside of one 9-inch cake pan and line the bottom with parchment or waxed paper. Butter the paper, and dust the entire pan with cocoa powder. Tap out the excess and set the pan aside.

○ In a medium bowl, sift together the 1 cup of cocoa powder, the flour, baking powder, and salt and set aside. In the bowl of a stand mixer fitted with a paddle, cream the butter and sugar at medium-high speed until light and fluffy (or use a handheld mixer). Add the eggs, one at a time, beating after each addition, until fully incorporated. Add the vanilla, and reduce the mixer speed to low. Gradually add the flour mixture, alternating with the sour cream, ending with the flour mixture. Using a rubber spatula, gently fold in the chocolate chunks and cherries.

○ Spread the batter into the prepared pan. Tap it firmly on the countertop to force out any large air bubbles. Bake until a toothpick inserted in the center comes out clean, about 35 to 40 minutes, turning the pan midway through baking. (You may have to poke the cake a few times to avoid testing a chocolate chunk.)

○ Remove from the oven and allow the cake to cool 10 minutes in the pan. Invert onto a cooling rack, turn right side up, and allow the cake to cool completely.

○ If you are frosting the cake, prep the cake stand or serving platter first by placing about four 3-inch-wide strips of waxed or parchment paper (foil will do in a pinch) around the edges, leaving the center of the stand empty. This keeps the surface clean. Place a dab of ganache in the center to anchor the bottom layer of the cake.

○ Slice the cake in half horizontally and place the bottom layer on the cake stand. Using an offset icing spatula cover the cake half with a layer of the ganache. Place the top layer on top and continue to spread the ganache over the cake until completely covered.

SERVES 8

SWEET TREAT

I like to invite everyone over after the movies or a concert. Although the desserts are the main draw, I also put out cheeses and nuts for the rare friend who doesn't have a sweet tooth. If you haven't had time to bake, here are some quick ways to indulge.

TOASTED LEFTOVER CAKE WITH CARAMELIZED FRUIT This works well with leftover Brown Sugar Angel Food Cake (page 130), or purchased pound cake. Earlier in the day combine ⅓ cup of dark brown sugar with 3 tablespoons of unsalted butter over high heat. When the sugar has melted, stir in 2 cups of pineapple chunks. Or try peeled and sliced apples or pears, and cook until the fruit is soft and the sugar is caramelized. Pair it with ice cream or crushed berries if you'd like, add a squeeze of lemon, and serve over slices of toasted cake.

DRESSED-UP ICE CREAM Experiment beyond mixing in the usual chopped candies. Soften the ice cream in the microwave or in a mixer. You can do this with everyone around or prepare it ahead of time and refreeze the ice cream. For example, simmer ½ teaspoon of saffron and 1 teaspoon of sugar or honey in ¼ cup of milk or heavy cream for 1 minute. Stir into vanilla ice cream and serve over sliced apricots, fresh or dried, for an adult dessert. Or whiz a few cups of berries and 1 tablespoon of sugar or honey in the food processor or blender. Mix into the ice cream, and serve drizzled with more honey and berries.

CHOCOLATE Set out a few chunks of good, quality chocolate and a dull but strong knife for self-service (although some kids, and parents, will need monitoring).

SWEET TREATS MENU

- LAUREN'S LEMON SQUARES (PAGE 125) WITH RASPBERRIES
- CHOCOLATE CHERRY CHUNK CAKE (PAGE 122)
- HONEY AND LIME FRUIT SALAD (PAGE 121)
- RUGGIES (PAGE 132)
- COCONUT TARTLETS WITH LIME CURD (PAGES 135 AND 131)

◦ KIDS IN THE KITCHEN ◦

Kids of most any age can help prepare the cake pan, measure the ingredients, sift the dry ingredients, help to fold the chocolate chunks and cherries, and frost. Older kids can learn how to operate the stand mixer under supervision, and help slice the cake.

SOUR CREAM GANACHE

This is my dream chocolate recipe, which I tinkered with in cooking school and appreciate even more now because of its versatility. It's simple, yet adds a sophisticated touch to a cake, with the tangy flavor of the sour cream and the bitter notes of the chocolate. You can pour it over a cake immediately after combining the ingredients for a shiny sheen, or let it sit a bit until it's thick enough to spread. It's delicious over cupcakes as well as on the Chocolate Cherry Chunk Cake (page 122). Or spoon into the Coconut Tartlets (page 135). When it's completely firm, you can form spoonfuls into balls and roll in cocoa powder or confectioners' sugar for truffles.

12 ounces bittersweet chocolate, chopped

2 tablespoons light corn syrup

2 tablespoons unsalted butter at room temperature

1¼ cups sour cream at room temperature (see Note)

○ Combine the chocolate, corn syrup, and butter in either the top of a double boiler or in a microwave-safe bowl. Heat over simmering water until the chocolate and butter melt, stirring occasionally, or if using the microwave, cover the bowl and heat on high for 35 seconds, then stir. If not fully melted, return to the microwave and continue to cook and stir in 5-second intervals until the mixture is melted.

○ Stir in the sour cream and let sit at room temperature until thick enough to spread, about ½ hour.

○ Let the ganache sit for ½ hour and use the leftovers for truffles.

YIELDS ENOUGH TO FROST ONE CAKE, OR ONE DOZEN CUPCAKES, OR ONE RECIPE COCONUT TARTLETS

NOTE If you forgot to take out the sour cream in advance, warm it in the microwave for 10 to 15 seconds at high heat, stir, and test for warmth. Return to the microwave at 5-second intervals until it reaches room temperature. This helps prevent the chocolate from becoming lumpy. If you do end up with lumps, you can strain the chocolate mixture, pressing with a rubber spatula.

○ **KIDS IN THE KITCHEN** ○

Younger kids can help measure, prepare the double boiler off the heat, and help frost the cake and make truffles. Older ones can also help chop the chocolate under supervision.

LAUREN'S LEMON SQUARES

Don't bypass these because they seem too pedestrian. Believe me, they're not! This is one of my signature desserts—a no-fail crowd-pleaser, and they freeze beautifully. In fact, I even bought an electric juicer because I make them so much. The kids can have fun helping you press the dough into the pans, too. Cut them into bite-size pieces and serve them on a cake stand with powdered sugar and raspberries to make them look a bit fancier.

FOR THE SHORTBREAD

2¼ cups all-purpose flour

½ cup sugar

1 cup (2 sticks) plus 2 tablespoons unsalted butter, cut in small pieces and chilled

FOR THE LEMON TOPPING

5 tablespoons all-purpose flour

2 cups sugar

4 eggs

¾ cup fresh lemon juice

Confectioners' sugar for garnish

Fresh raspberries for garnish (optional)

○ Preheat the oven to 350 degrees F.

○ To make the shortbread, in a food processor, pulse the flour and sugar to combine. Remove the lid, distribute the butter evenly over the flour mixture, and pulse until just combined. Press the mixture into the bottom of a 9-by-13-inch pan. Bake for 20 minutes, turning the pan halfway through baking.

○ While the shortbread is baking, make the lemon topping. In a small bowl, whisk together the flour and sugar. In a large bowl, lightly whisk the eggs and gently whisk the flour mixture into the eggs. Add the lemon juice, taking care not to create too many air bubbles. Pour the topping over the hot shortbread (I usually do this while the pan is still sitting on the oven rack, so it's not a wobbly mess). Bake for 20 more minutes, carefully turning halfway through baking. Do not worry if the top cracks slightly.

○ Cool completely in the pan and cut into squares or triangles. Dust with confectioners' sugar, and pile on a cake pedestal. You may need to add more confectioners' sugar if assembled far in advance of serving. A few scattered fresh raspberries add a nice pop of color.

MAKES 24 TWO-INCH SQUARES

NOTE If freezing, do not cut the squares before placing in freezer. Allow them to cool in the pan and wrap tightly in plastic and then foil. The night before or morning of serving, defrost on the counter and cut to the desired size.

○ **KIDS IN THE KITCHEN** ○

Most kids can help measure the ingredients, pulse in the food processor under supervision, and press the dough into the pan. They can squeeze the lemons, whisk the topping ingredients, and help with serving by piling the lemon squares, dusting with confectioners' sugar, and garnishing with raspberries.

FAIRY-TALE BIRTHDAY CAKE

No matter how many trucks or plastic tool kits you give your daughter, there comes a day when you just have to stand aside and let the princess in her take over. Resistance is futile; just go with it. For Natasha's third birthday, I re-created the fairy-tale magic of a ball-gown cake I had secretly been dying to make.

This version has my favorite vanilla cake with clouds of whipped cream rather than the expected buttercream. If you're talented with a pastry bag, by all means, use your favorite buttercream recipe and go wild! However, I find that the whipped cream is just as impressive, and can cover a multitude of mistakes, especially once the shower of candied sugar and flowers hit the frosting to make your creation the belle of the ball. Natasha was bewitched into a rare moment of silence!

VANILLA BIRTHDAY CAKE

1 cup (2 sticks) unsalted butter at room temperature

1⅔ cups sugar

4 eggs

1½ teaspoons vanilla extract

1½ cups self-rising cake flour (see Notes)

1½ cups all-purpose flour

1 cup milk

CLOUD FROSTING

3 pints heavy cream

1 teaspoon vanilla extract

2½ cups confectioners' sugar

Colored sugar, edible dragées, candied flowers, or other sugar decorations

SPECIAL EQUIPMENT: one 9-inch round cake pan, 2 inches high; one 3-quart ovenproof metal bowl, 9 inches in diameter; 1 new doll

○ Preheat the oven to 350 degrees F. Arrange the oven racks to accommodate the bowl and cake pan. To begin the cake, prepare the pan. Butter the cake pan, line the bottom with parchment or waxed paper, butter the paper, and flour the pan. Tap out the excess and set the pan aside. Butter and flour the metal bowl.

○ In the bowl of a stand mixer, cream the butter on medium speed until light and smooth. Add the sugar gradually and beat for 3 minutes, until fluffy. Add the eggs, one at a time, fully incorporating each one before adding the next. Add the vanilla and mix.

○ In small bowl, whisk together the flours. On low speed, add a third of the flour to the butter mixture and beat to incorporate. Next, add ⅓ cup of the milk. Continue alternating between the two, ending with the flour. Take care not to overmix.

○ Fill the 2-inch-high cake pan with a third of the batter. This will be the base of the cake. Pour the remaining batter into the prepared bowl. Put both in the oven. Bake the cake for 25 to 30 minutes, or until a toothpick inserted into the center comes away clean. Bake the bowl cake for about 1 hour and 15 to 20 minutes, and use a longer skewer or the point of a knife to test for doneness. Turn the cakes midway through baking.

○ Cool the cakes in the pan and bowl for about 10 minutes. Carefully invert the cakes and transfer to cooling racks to cool fully before assembling. Use a narrow, flexible offset spatula to help release the bowl cake. The widest part of the bowl cake should be resting on the rack.

○ Meanwhile, prepare the doll. Remove the clothing and pop the legs off at the hips. They usually go back on easily, but you don't want to do this with a favorite doll!

○ Pull back the hair and wipe the doll clean. Cover the doll's head, hips, and bottom with plastic wrap. You will be decorating the doll's torso and bust, so leave unwrapped.

➡ CONTINUED

➥ CONTINUED

○ Clear a spot in the fridge and check the height of the doll for clearance. You can decorate the doll at the last minute and insert into the cake before serving if you don't have the room, but leave enough time.

◉ To prepare the frosting, combine the cream and vanilla in the bowl of a stand mixer fitted with the whisk. Whip the cream on high, and gradually add the confectioners' sugar. Whip for about 1 minute, until stiff peaks have formed.

○ To assemble the cake, place four 3-inch-wide strips of waxed or parchment paper (foil will do in a pinch) around the edges of the cake stand or serving platter, leaving the center of the stand empty. This will keep your surface clean.

○ Using a large serrated bread or cake knife, slice the round cake base layer in half horizontally into 2 layers. Slice the bowl cake horizontally as well.

◉ Place a dab of frosting in the center of the stand to anchor the cake, and place the bottom layer of the base on the cake stand. Cover with frosting. Top with the second layer of the base and frost all of the cake. Top with the widest layer of the bowl cake, and frost the layer. Top with the last layer, but do not frost the top of the cake yet. You can add extra frosting later if the edges of the bowl layer don't exactly match.

◉ Measure the doll around the hips. With a long, thin knife (not serrated) score a circle on the top of the cake, in the center, to fit the doll. It will probably be about 1 inch in diameter. With the knife, cut around the circle, 1 inch deep. Remove the cake plug with a small offset spatula or a spoon. Don't make the hole too deep; the doll shouldn't sink down into the center. If this happens, simply return some of the plug. You will pipe or decorate a bustier, or top, of the dress, so the doll should be waist high in the cake.

○ Place the doll in the cake, and finish the top of the cake, and the doll's bodice. If you are not piping, you may want to use a line of dragées (silver decorating candies; make sure they are edible) or colored candies to make a beaded neckline. Any of these will keep the top of the dress straight and the frosting in place.

○ Dust and decorate away. Keep the cake refrigerated until 15 minutes before serving. I suggest cutting the first slice and then removing the doll and continuing to slice. If the child is very young, do this away from the party table as the kids may become upset by the legless doll.

SERVES 10

NOTES If you don't have self-rising cake flour, combine 2¼ teaspoons of baking powder and ½ teaspoon of salt with 1½ cups of all-purpose flour.

Do not panic if the bowl cake is a bit dented or cracked when transferring onto the cake rack. The frosting will hide any imperfections.

The cake recipe can also be used to make 2 dozen cupcakes; test for doneness after 20 minutes.

DANGER MOUNTAIN VARIATION Mathias is obsessed with all things scary, so here's his version. Do not make a hole in the top of the cake; simply serve it as a mountain. Replace the princess doll with an action figure hanging off the side of the mountain, or a large dinosaur or other creature making its ascent. Make a chocolate mousse frosting by following the frosting recipe, but first melt 8 ounces of bittersweet or semisweet chocolate in the microwave for 20 to 30 seconds. Whisk in an additional ⅓ cup heavy cream until smooth. Whip the 3 pints of heavy cream as directed in the recipe, but add the chocolate mixture toward the end, along with the last of the confectioners' sugar, until smooth.

Frost the cake and top the cake with store-bought gummy worms, candied "rocks," and either "bad guys" or more creatures. Set the table with cut geodes and big rocks to complete the illusion!

○ KIDS IN THE KITCHEN ○

Kids of almost any age can help measure the ingredients, cut the softened butter with a plastic knife, prepare the cake pan, and help frost and decorate the cake. Older kids can learn how to operate the stand mixer under supervision.

If you are serving extra cupcakes to decorate for an activity, have the kids arrange the colored sugars in bowls and help you add food coloring to individual bowls of whipped cream for colored frosting.

BROWN SUGAR ANGEL FOOD CAKE

Not only is this cake yummy; it's also a hands-on science experiment that the kids, and probably some adults, will be talking about long after dessert is over. The cloudlike egg whites and the traditional way of cooling the cake—upside down over a wine bottle—invite a lot of questions that are fun to answer. If the kids are old enough, turn the kitchen session into a real science class and have them find an explanation for why the eggs expand while being beaten and while baking in the oven. In fact, it's fun to have everything premeasured and make the cake when everyone arrives. Don't worry about what to do with all those leftover yolks; see page 131.

1½ cups firmly packed light brown sugar

1¼ cups sifted cake flour

10 egg whites at room temperature

1 teaspoon almond extract (see Notes)

1½ teaspoons cream of tartar

1 teaspoon salt

SPECIAL EQUIPMENT: one 10-inch angel food cake pan, preferably with removable bottom, with no traces of grease

○ Preheat the oven to 350 degrees F.

○ Pulse the brown sugar in a food processor 5 or so times. Remove half of the sugar and set aside. Add the sifted cake flour and pulse 5 times. Set aside.

○ In the bowl of a stand mixer fitted with a whisk attachment, or with a hand-held mixer, beat the egg whites and almond extract together on high speed just until foamy. Add the cream of tartar and salt and whip until soft peaks form. (The eggs will curl over slightly when lifted with a spoon.)

○ Remove the bowl from the mixer. Sprinkle the reserved ¾ cup of brown sugar over the egg-white mixture and let the sugar dissolve slightly for a few seconds. Using a rubber spatula, gently fold in the dissolved sugar, about 3 folds. Gently fold the sugar and flour mixture into the bowl, in batches.

○ Using a spatula, gently pour the batter into a 10-inch, ungreased angel food cake pan. Bake for 35 to 40 minutes, or until a toothpick inserted in the center comes out clean. Invert the pan over a wine bottle and cool completely; otherwise it will collapse and deflate from its own weight.

SERVES 8 TO 10

NOTES Omit the almond extract and increase the sugar by 1/4 cup if you are aware of nut allergies.

The slightest bit of yolk in the whites will prevent the whites from reaching their full volume. Separate each egg into two smaller bowls, one for the white, one for the yolk. Then add the white to the other whites so you don't ruin the batter. See Notes on page 138 for more information about egg whites.

○ KIDS IN THE KITCHEN ○

Buy an extra dozen or so eggs and set up two bowls per child, or for each pair of kids. Have them practice cracking and separating the eggs, with their (clean) hands or a store-bought egg-separating tool if you prefer. Most kids can also help measure the ingredients, sift the flour, pulse the sugar (under supervision), beat the egg whites under supervision, fold the flour and sugar into the egg whites, and pour the batter into the tube pan.

LIME CURD

I love lime curd. A batch this size gives you something delicious to do with the yolks left over from the Brown Sugar Angel Food Cake on the facing page. You can cut this recipe in half, though, and have it anytime. It's great spooned inside the Coconut Tartlets (page 135). Child labor comes in handy when the curd needs to be stirred in a figure eight for 15 minutes to prevent scrambled eggs. You may need several volunteers for when boredom and arm cramps set in.

12 limes

10 egg yolks

1½ cups sugar

½ cup (1 stick) unsalted butter, cut into tablespoons

○ Zest 4 of the limes. Juice the limes and the remaining 8 limes. Measure 1½ cups of juice for this recipe. In a large saucepan over medium heat, whisk together the egg yolks, lime juice and zest, and sugar. Switch to a wooden spoon and stir constantly, in a figure eight and around the sides of the pan, for 10 to 15 minutes, until the mixture coats the back of the spoon. When you trace a line through the curd that is coating the back of the spoon, it should remain visible, rather than disappear.

○ Remove from the heat and stir in the butter, 1 tablespoon at a time. Strain to remove the zest if desired, or any lumps that may have formed. Transfer the lime curd to a bowl, cover the surface with plastic wrap, and chill until firm, about 3 hours.

MAKES ABOUT 3½ CUPS

NOTES A Microplane rasp works fast and gives you nice thin bits of zest.

TRIFLES Have the kids make their own trifles with leftover angel food or store-bought pound cake, Lime Curd, whipped cream, and raspberries.

LEMON CURD Substitute the zest of 2 lemons and the juice of 5 lemons for the lime juice and zest. Increase the butter by 3 tablespoons. The method is the same.

○ **KIDS IN THE KITCHEN** ○

Most kids can help juice the limes, and cut the butter with plastic knives. Older kids can zest the limes, stir away, add the tablespoons of butter, and help strain the curd.

RUGGIES (AUNT LINDA'S RUGALACH)

These sandy, crescent roll–shaped, traditional Jewish cookies come from my Aunt Linda, who went well beyond the traditional jam and nut fillings and started using wacky candy chunks. She used to sell them years ago, and kept her recipe under lock and key. I finally got it out of her on a recent trip to Texas, but only on condition that I help her make hundreds of them for a friend's birthday. It took five hours!

FOR THE DOUGH

1½ pounds cream cheese at room temperature

1½ pounds (6 sticks) unsalted butter at room temperature

1½ teaspoons salt

6¾ cups all-purpose flour

TO FILL AND ROLL

1½ pounds each of about 4 favorite candies, such as Rolos, Heath bars, M&M's, yogurt raisins, or chocolate-covered raisins (see Notes)

One 15-ounce jar raspberry or apricot jam

2 cups walnuts, finely ground (see Notes)

1 cup granulated sugar

1 teaspoon ground cinnamon

About 3 cups confectioners' sugar

○ To prepare the dough, use a stand mixer fitted with a paddle or a very large bowl and a handheld mixer to cream together the cream cheese and the butter. (If your mixer is small you may find this easier to do in 2 batches.) In a separate bowl, whisk the salt into the flour. Mixing on the lowest speed, add the flour to the mixing bowl 1 cup at a time, until a creamy dough forms. Split the dough into 4 pieces and shape them into rounds. Wrap each one in plastic and refrigerate for 1 hour, or freeze for 20 minutes.

○ To prepare the filling, use a food processor to pulse each candy separately into coarse chunks, like those you find mixed into ice cream. Or place the candies in plastic bags and crack and roll with a rolling pin. If using apricot jam, blend in the food processor or strain so that no lumps of apricot remain.

○ In a separate bowl, mix the walnuts, granulated sugar, and cinnamon and set aside.

○ Preheat the oven to 325 degrees F.

○ Tape waxed paper or parchment over your work surface, or use a counter-sized silicone mat. Remove one dough round at a time from the refrigerator. Sprinkle a bit of flour on your rolling surface and sprinkle about 2 tablespoons of the walnut and sugar mixture over the flour.

Now, while no sane person would make hundreds at a time, baking rugalach is a great activity for a birthday party. It makes a big mess, but it's loads of fun and once the cookies are done, they get dropped into the take-home goody bags—hurray! You can also make a batch of the dough the night before and keep it in the refrigerator. Linda's tip is to tape down waxed paper over the entire surface of your kitchen table; you'll need a very large work space. This makes a big batch, but you can easily halve this recipe.

○ Gently roll out the dough into a ¼-inch-thick circle about 8 to 10 inches in diameter, pressing the walnut mixture into the dough as you roll. Spread a very thin layer of jam over the rolled dough. Cover the entire surface with chopped candy and sprinkle with some of the walnut mixture. Gently press the fillings into the dough with your hands or a large spatula.

○ With a pizza cutter or knife, divide the dough into 16 to 18 pie-shaped wedges about 1 to 1½ inches wide. Pick up the outside edge and tightly roll a rugalach towards the center, pressing and tucking the tip under and the fillings back in if they are pushed out. Sprinkle with more walnut sugar. Place on a baking sheet lined with parchment paper or a silicone mat. Continue rolling the dough until you have used it up. Repeat with the remaining pieces of dough. (You will have to do this in batches.)

○ Bake for 20 to 25 minutes, or until the rugalach are golden brown and the filling is bubbling. Transfer to a cooling rack.

MAKES ABOUT 65–70 COOKIES

NOTES Pulse the walnuts in a food processor until they are finely ground; be careful not to turn them into a paste.

This recipe allows for extra candy, as some always mysteriously disappears during the filling and rolling.

○ **KIDS IN THE KITCHEN** ○

Older kids can measure the ingredients, mix the dough, and, under supervision, cut the ruggies with either pizza wheels or plastic knives, depending on their age. Everyone else can roll out the dough (with help as needed), crumble candy, sprinkle and roll the ruggies, and top with walnut sugar.

COCONUT TARTLETS AND ICE CREAM SANDWICHES

I am mad for coconut, for both savory (see page 107) and sweet courses. These tartlets, with thumb impressions in their centers, are super-easy, and kids can make them without much supervision. Bake them in minimuffin tins and fill them with sorbet, chocolate ganache with raspberries, or Lime Curd (page 131), or just about anything you want. Or try the cookie variation below for crunchy, coconut-y ice cream sandwiches.

FOR THE TARTLETS

½ cup sugar

2 egg whites

2 cups sweetened shredded coconut

FOR THE GANACHE

1½ cups heavy cream

8 ounces bittersweet or semisweet chocolate, finely chopped

2 pints raspberries

○ Preheat the oven to 325 degrees F.

○ Butter a minimuffin tin very well. Applying melted butter with a silicone brush is the most efficient way.

◉ In a large bowl, whisk together the sugar and the egg whites until the egg whites are foamy. Switch to a wooden spoon or spatula and mix in the coconut.

○ Spoon about a tablespoon of the mixture into each muffin cup, and using your fingers, press to fill in the bottom and sides of the cup and make an indentation with your thumb.

○ Bake for about 25 minutes, turning the tin halfway through baking. The tartlets puff a bit when baking, but you can deflate them with a spoon afterward.

○ Let cool for 5 to 10 minutes. Run a small spatula or knife around the sides and remove. They may stick a bit; simply push them back into shape. Cool completely on a rack.

○ Meanwhile, make the ganache. In a saucepan over medium-high heat, bring the cream to a simmer. Remove from the heat, add the chocolate, and stir until completely melted. Let cool for about 5 minutes, and fill the tartlets. If left to sit, the ganache will firm up, so rewarm in a double boiler if you've made it in advance. Let the tartlets set for about 30 minutes, and top each one with a raspberry.

MAKES 2 DOZEN TARTLETS

CHOCOLATE COCONUT TARTLETS

Sift in 2 teaspoons of cocoa powder before baking. Or, divide a batch in half and sift 1 teaspoon into half a batch for two flavors: plain and chocolate.

COCONUT ICE CREAM SANDWICHES

Increase the sugar in the tartlet recipe to a total of 1¼ cups. Form the mixture into 10 balls and place the cookies 2 inches apart on a baking sheet lined with buttered parchment paper or a silicone mat. Gently flatten the balls, then bake as instructed above. Let cool slightly, use a thin spatula to transfer the cookies to a cooling rack, and cool completely. To make sandwiches, beat the ice cream or sorbet in a stand mixer to soften a bit. Spread an inch or so of the ice cream on each sandwich bottom, and top with another cookie.

MAKES 4 SANDWICHES

CHOCOLATE PLAY DOUGH

What says "playdate" better than play dough? This requires little more than melting some chocolate the night before and a place where you can make a mess the next day. When handled gently, the dough can be rolled and cut into shapes with cookie cutters and left to firm up to make edible holiday ornaments, chocolate Valentines, or decorations for cakes or cupcakes. These are more of a candy treat than a true dessert, but it's still a delish way to amuse the kids on a snow day or when you're just plain outnumbered.

1 ½ pounds semisweet chocolate chips or coarsely chopped chocolate

⅔ cup light corn syrup

1 to 2 cups cocoa powder, plus extra to prevent sticking (see Note)

○ Line a large rimmed baking sheet or roasting pan with waxed paper, parchment, or a silicone sheet.

○ Melt the chocolate in the top of a double boiler, or put in a microwave-safe bowl, cover, and microwave on high for 1 to 2 minutes, checking and stirring in 30-second intervals. It's important to stir if you are using chips because they hold their shape even while partially melted. Add the corn syrup, and carefully stir the mixture with a spatula.

○ Transfer the mixture to the prepared baking sheet and refrigerate overnight.

○ To play with the dough, cut the dough into portions and give one to each child. Set out an array of rolling pins, cookie cutters, and decorating candies. Sprinkle the cocoa powder lightly on the dough and work surface and lightly knead the dough as needed to prevent sticking.

○ The play dough will dry out overnight. For ornaments, you can pierce a hole, let the ornament dry, and tie a string through the hole. Or cut out designs and place on top of frosted cupcakes or a birthday cake while the play dough is still moist.

SERVES 4 PLAYERS

NOTE Here's one time I don't recommend using expensive cocoa powder! The dough tends to become sticky from the heat of excited little hands, so you will need to use plenty of cocoa powder to help prevent sticking.

○ **KIDS IN THE KITCHEN** ○

Since the dough is made in advance, this recipe is ideal for kids who are staying overnight. Older ones can melt the chocolate. Everyone else can help prepare the pan, measure the ingredients, and of course, play.

CHOCOLATE TOASTED ALMOND ICE CREAM

When I was researching canned desserts for a TV program, I came across dozens of recipes and came up with this simple one for ice cream. If you don't add the almonds, it's a "no-machine ice cream!"

1 can (12 ounces) evaporated milk

1 can (14 ounces) sweetened condensed milk

1 cup heavy cream

1 cup slivered almonds, toasted (see Note on page 111)

1 teaspoon vanilla extract

½ cup cocoa powder

Combine all the ingredients in a food processor and pulse a few times. The almond chunks should remain coarse. Pour into a freezer-safe bowl, or a loaf pan, which makes scooping it simpler. Press plastic wrap onto the surface to prevent crystallization. Freeze for at least 6 hours, or overnight.

SERVES 4

VARIATIONS   The possibilities are endless—whatever you can dream up. Omit the cocoa powder for a true toasted almond scoop. Or make a fancy version with different extracts, or ground cinnamon, or frozen berries. Add a pinch of saffron softened in a bit of warm water for a sophisticated treat. Or, if you want your kids to think you are a total rock star, stir in chopped candy bars and marshmallows.

○ KIDS IN THE KITCHEN ○

Most kids can help measure, pulse ingredients in a food processor, pour the ice cream into a container, and scoop out for serving. If you like, divide the batch into portions and let the kids flavor and freeze their own.

SNOWBALL SUNDAES AND OTHER MERINGUE DELIGHTS

I am obsessed with meringues. They are ethereal, sugary, and incredibly versatile. Start with the basic meringue Snowball Sundae recipe or shape into one large Cloud (see facing page). By varying the size and shape and slightly adjusting the baking time, you can have a parade of desserts. The Snowballs take the place of profiteroles; I find them easier and addictively sweet. Let the kids smash them slightly and top with a scoop of ice cream. If you like, top with a drizzle of Sour Cream Ganache (page 124). My kids love to make smaller meringue Kisses and give these for Valentine's gifts, tied in cellophane bundles with lots of ribbons. Sweet heaven!

6 egg whites

1½ cups sugar

½ teaspoon vanilla extract

1 quart ice cream, or 2 to 3 pints of different flavors, for serving

2 cups chocolate sauce or 2 cups berries for serving

Whipped cream for serving

1½ cups chopped nuts

○ Preheat the oven to 350 degrees F.

○ Line a baking sheet with parchment or a silicone sheet.

○ In the bowl of a large stand mixer fitted with a whisk, beat the egg whites on high speed until soft peaks form. Add the sugar slowly while beating, a few spoonfuls at a time, until the meringue is stiff and shiny. Add the vanilla and beat to incorporate evenly.

○ Using a large spoon, drop large rounds of meringue the size of a snowball onto the baking sheet, about 2 inches apart. Lower the oven temperature to 300 degrees F. Bake the meringues for 1 hour to 1 hour and 15 minutes. The meringues should feel firm outside and slightly soft inside, and be pale ivory in color. Turn off the oven, open the oven door, and allow to cool. Using a spatula, transfer to a cooling rack.

○ To serve, lightly smash the top of each meringue, add a scoop of ice cream, top with chocolate sauce or fruit, a dollop of whipped cream, and a shower of nuts.

SERVES 8 TO 10

NOTES There are a few rules that make life with meringues a bit easier:

Don't try these on a humid day, as the humidity will make the eggs weep liquid.

It's easier to separate the yolks and whites when the egg is cold. Take care because the tiniest bit of yolk will wilt a batch of whites.

Let the whites get to room temperature before beating for the most volume.

Make certain the bowl you use for beating the egg whites is clean, without a trace of oil or fat.

If making in advance, wrap the fully cooled meringues in foil—not plastic—to prevent them from becoming soggy.

MERINGUE CLOUD

This is a slightly less chewy version of a Pavlova dessert. Prepare the meringue as instructed above, but spoon into 1 large mounded oval about 10 by 5 inches on the prepared baking sheet. Bake for 1½ hours, remove from the oven, and allow to cool on the baking sheet. Carefully loosen the bottom with a thin spatula and transfer to a serving platter. Cover with whipped cream and raspberries or black-berries, or spread with Lime Curd (page 131), whipped cream, and a handful of raspberries.

SERVES 6 TO 8

MERINGUE KISSES

Drop tablespoons of meringue onto the prepared baking sheet in the shape of kisses. Or cut the corner off a large plastic bag, fill with meringue, and squeeze out the kisses. Sprinkle with colored sugar and small candy hearts or any edible decorations, and bake at 300 degrees F for about 1 hour and 15 minutes. Turn off the oven, open the oven door, and allow to cool. If packaging as a gift be sure to use cellophane or foil because plastic bags may make the kisses soggy.

MAKES 60 TO 70 KISSES

BROWN SUGAR–ALMOND MERINGUES

These have an almost burnt-sugar flavor, richer than the typical meringue. Make any version (Snowball, Cloud, or Kisses) as instructed above, but substitute light brown sugar for the white sugar, and add 1 cup of toasted sliced almonds or chopped toasted hazelnuts.

CHOCOLATE CHUNK MERINGUES

For serious chocaholics. Sift ¼ cup of cocoa powder over the stiff meringue and fold in 4 ounces of finely chopped bittersweet chocolate. (If using semisweet, reduce the sugar by ¼ cup.) Make into Snowballs, a Cloud, or Kisses.

◦ KIDS IN THE KITCHEN ◦

Buy an extra dozen eggs and set up two bowls per child, or for each pair of kids. Have them practice cracking and separating the eggs with their (clean) hands or a store-bought egg-separating tool if you prefer. They can wipe the mixing bowl with a bit of lemon juice or vinegar to remove any traces of oil, help beat the egg whites (with supervision), slowly add the sugar, and shape or pipe the meringues. They can also help set up a sundae bar, or garnish the meringue cloud, or pack the kisses if giving as gifts.

STICKY TOFFEE PUDDING

This British classic for the sugar addict comes to me from my friend chef Lee Hanson of the hip McNally restaurant empire—Balthazar, Pastis, and the late-night joint Schiller's Liquor Bar, where they serve these puddings. This is comfort food of the sweetest order; just don't expect custard. It is a cakelike baked pudding. Toffee pudding is probably a bit rich to have after a big dinner, so save it for the finale of an Asian meal or when friends come over after the movies.

I've made the puddings easier, too. They're baked in a muffin tin instead of restaurant-issue ramekins. The sauce is made on the stove top while they bake. In fact, you can make the entire dessert, sauce and all, in advance and stash them in the fridge for up to 3 days. When you're ready to serve them, just pop 'em in the oven for 15 minutes. That's it!

5 ounces pitted dates (about 1 cup)

½ cup boiling water

1½ cups all-purpose flour

½ teaspoon baking powder

¼ teaspoon baking soda

5 tablespoons unsalted butter at room temperature

1 cup dark brown sugar

2 eggs

Toffee Sauce (page 142)

Vanilla ice cream for serving

○ Preheat the oven to 350 degrees F. Butter a 12-cup muffin tin.

○ Combine the dates and water in a small saucepan and bring to a boil over high heat. Simmer until most of the water is evaporated, leaving a little less than one-quarter of the liquid. In a food processor or blender, purée the remaining water and dates until smooth. Keep the top on the appliance so the mixture stays warm while you make the rest of the batter.

○ In a medium bowl, whisk the flour with the baking powder and baking soda and set aside.

○ In a stand mixer fitted with the paddle attachment, or with a handheld mixer, cream the butter and sugar at medium speed until fluffy, about 2 to 3 minutes. Add the eggs, one at a time, fully incorporating after each addition. Scrape down the sides of the bowl with a spatula as needed.

○ Add the flour mixture gradually to the batter and mix on medium speed until the flour is just incorporated. Add the date purée in 2 batches, making sure the dates are fully incorporated before adding the next batch.

○ Spoon the batter into the muffin cups. They should be three-quarters full; do not overfill. Bake for 20 to 23 minutes, until a toothpick inserted in the center comes out clean. It may be slightly sticky if you hit a date, so retest. Let cool for 5 minutes in the pans and then transfer to a cooling rack to cool completely.

○ Make the Toffee Sauce while the muffins are baking.

○ After the puddings have cooled to room temperature, cut off a thin slice from the top of each cake so that it is even and the pudding will sit flat when it is plated upside down. (Snack on the slices while you and your helpers are cooking.) Next, slice each cake in half horizontally through the middle.

○ Spoon about 2 tablespoons of sauce in the bottom of each muffin cup. Return each bottom cake layer back to a muffin cup on top of the sauce. Spoon in 2 more tablespoons of sauce over each layer, place the top of each cake over the sauce, and top with more sauce until completely covered.

○ At this point the puddings can be wrapped in the muffin tin and refrigerated for up to 3 days.

○ About 30 minutes before you are ready to serve, preheat the oven to 400 degrees F.

○ Place the muffin tin on a foil-lined rimmed baking sheet, as the mixture will bubble over. Heat the cakes until the sauce bubbles, about 10 minutes. Remove each pudding with a small spatula and invert onto a dessert plate, taking care not to burn yourself with the hot Toffee Sauce. Serve with more sauce and vanilla ice cream.

SERVES 12

○ **KIDS IN THE KITCHEN** ○

Most kids can measure the ingredients, butter the muffin tin, pulse the dates in the food processor (under supervision), and carefully add the ingredients to the mixer. They can also help fill the muffin cups. Once the puddings and toffee sauce are cool enough to handle, they can help assemble the cakes in the muffin tin. After the puddings bake, older kids can help top the hot cakes with ice cream and serve.

TOFFEE SAUCE

I have made dozens of caramel and toffee sauces, but this version remains my favorite. Caramelizing the white sugar rather than taking a brown-sugar shortcut makes a big difference. Be sure to use a big saucepan so it can bubble away without spilling or burning. This is pretty much a "kids-out-of-the-kitchen" recipe because the sauce becomes dangerously hot. You will have some left over after you sauce the Toffee Pudding (page 140). We love it over Brown Sugar–Almond Meringue Snowball Sundaes with pineapple chunks (see variation, page 139).

2½ cups heavy cream

2 cups sugar

⅓ cup corn syrup

4 tablespoons unsalted butter

In a large saucepan over medium-high heat, combine 1¼ cups of the cream and the remaining ingredients. Cook for about 20 to 30 minutes, stirring frequently, until the mixture begins to turn a dark brown caramel color. This color changes fairly rapidly towards the end of the cooking time. You can take the mixture on and off the heat to control the temperature and rate of cooking. Remove from the heat and let cool for 15 minutes.

Meanwhile, bring the remaining 1¼ cups of cream to a simmer in a small saucepan or heat in the microwave. Stir into the partially cooled sauce. If there are some lumps of crystallized sugar, simply strain the sauce.

Cool the sauce completely and cover with waxed paper or plastic wrap. It will keep, refrigerated, for up to 1 week.

MAKES ABOUT 2 1/2 CUPS

○ KIDS OUT OF THE KITCHEN ○

Keep them out until they are old enough to understand how hot and dangerous the sugar mixture can be. However, let them look at the initial color of the sauce, and spoon some on a white plate during cooking at various times so they can see how the color changes, and taste the difference once the sauce has cooled.

⦿ MAD HATTER TEA PARTY ⦿

A few of my producer pals live pretty far away, so I organize a tea party playdate for them that can be served at any time of the day. No one needs to go crazy trying to arrive by a set time. We all know what it's like to travel with kids—the irregular nap schedules, unexpected toddler tantrums, and late soccer games. So really, who needs another thing to stress about? Unlike kids, the scones will wait patiently, and they can be popped in the oven upon the weary moms' arrival. Or better yet, wait until the guests arrive and let the kids get messy putting them together while the moms get a chance to unwind!

This is a *very* relaxed tea. Have the tea sandwich fixings set out as a bar to mix and match, or have your kids make them before the guests arrive. One of my favorite things to serve are eggs cooked with tea and herbs. The kids love to peel these interestingly marbled eggs, which I tell them are dinosaur eggs, a great—albeit sneaky—way to encourage Mathias to eat eggs.

For the tea, buy a variety of loose teas, or make it simple and buy tea bags. Have the children smell the different varieties. They can taste them too, as long as they're decaffeinated. There are many great fruit-flavored teas that kids will enjoy without bouncing off the walls as they do on caffeine. It's also fun to have a map or globe handy so they can learn something about where tea comes from. You can get interesting sugars, too, like rock candy sticks or muscovado, a dark brown sugar. Or color your own sugar (see page 170), or put out an assortment of honeys to keep the sweet-obsessed tea partiers interested.

If there are new friends coming, you can buy plain white doilies to use as placemats, and have the kids color and decorate them with stickers and nametags. When the kids are finished with their sandwiches or scones, keep the fun and frivolity of a tea party going with simple craft projects. Stock up on sturdy restaurant or ovenproof teacups that the kids can decorate with paints or ceramic markers. Then they can use their creations to hold their desserts. A napkin-folding book and stacks of colored paper napkins are also great for keeping hands busy.

Make mini Brown Sugar Angel Food Cakes (page 130) for guests to take home. SiliconeZone makes a six-in-one tray. Or buy Farberware's minis to give away as favors.

MENU

- DINOSAUR EGGS
  In a large saucepan over medium-high heat, combine ½ cup of soy sauce, 3 cups of water, 1 cinnamon stick, 1 teaspoon Chinese five-spice powder, ½ teaspoon of brown sugar, and 3 black tea bags and bring to a boil. Add the eggs and simmer for 40 minutes. Allow to cool to room temperature, and chill. You can chill the eggs overnight in the liquid.

- LAUREN'S LEMON SQUARES (PAGE 125)

- CHERRY SCONES (PAGE 158)

- LIME CURD (PAGE 131) WITH WHIPPED CREAM, OR STORE-BOUGHT SORBETS

- FRUIT TEA OR WARM HONEY AND LEMON WATER WITH MINT SPRIGS (for kids: spoonful of honey, squeeze of lemon, and mint sprig mixed with warm water or decaffeinated fruit teas).

- TEA SANDWICHES
  Ham, butter, and fig or prune jam; PB and J cut into triangles like butterfly wings; smoked turkey, lettuce, and mayonnaise with sides buttered and dipped into sesame seeds.

PANNA COTTA WITH ROASTED BALSAMIC STRAWBERRIES AND PEPPER

This is really creamy Jell-O for grown-ups, not that children don't adore this, too. It's the perfect playdate dessert—not fussy, can be made a few days in advance, and delivers the excitement of a restaurant dessert. The process is simple. There are no eggs threatening to curdle, just basic simmering and stirring. You can experiment endlessly with variations. Try adding cinnamon or almond extract, or heating some cardamom seeds with the cream. Since the panna cotta is a bit rich, the slight acidity of the balsamic-splashed fruit and a few twists of pepper add just the right notes.

FOR THE PANNA COTTA

1½ teaspoons unflavored gelatin (½ envelope)

½ cup cold whole milk

1 cup heavy cream

¼ cup sugar

1 vanilla bean, or 1 teaspoon vanilla extract

FOR THE ROASTED STRAWBERRIES

1 quart strawberries, hulled and quartered

1 tablespoon balsamic vinegar

2 teaspoons dark brown sugar

1 tablespoon butter, quartered

Freshly ground pepper to taste

SPECIAL EQUIPMENT: four 8-ounce ramekins, or one 6-cup silicone muffin tray

○ Lightly butter the ramekins or muffin cups. Place the ramekins on a baking sheet for easy handling, and chill the ramekins or muffin tray in the refrigerator while you prepare the panna cotta.

○ In a medium bowl, combine the gelatin and ¼ cup of the milk. Stir gently and set aside.

○ In a medium saucepan over medium-high heat, combine the remaining ¼ cup of milk with the heavy cream and sugar and stir gently. If using the vanilla bean, split the bean in half lengthwise and scrape the tiny seeds from half of the pod into the saucepan, and add the half a pod as well. Do not add the vanilla extract yet.

○ Bring the cream to a simmer, but do not allow the mixture to boil. Gently whisk the hot liquid into the gelatin mixture. Remove the vanilla bean pod if you have used one. Allow this mixture to cool to room temperature. If you are in a rush, place the bowl inside of a larger one filled with ice and a bit of water and stir gently, taking care not to splash water into the cream mixture. Add the vanilla extract if you haven't used the vanilla bean.

○ Pour the mixture into the ramekins or muffin cups, and press a piece of plastic wrap on the surface of the cream to prevent a skin from forming. Refrigerate for at least 4 hours, or overnight.

○ Before serving, prepare the strawberries. Preheat the oven to 400 degrees F. Put the strawberries in a medium-size roasting pan or a 9-by-13-inch baking dish. Sprinkle with the balsamic vinegar, sugar, and butter, and toss. Roast for about 15 minutes, until the strawberries are soft and surrounded by juice. Season with a twist or two of freshly ground pepper.

○ To serve, gently run a small offset spatula or paring knife around the edges of each panna cotta to loosen it from its mold. Invert them onto individual dessert plates. Spoon some of the strawberries alongside or atop each panna cotta.

SERVES 4 TO 6

NOTES If you don't have enough ramekins, you can also use teacups. If you damage a panna cotta while unmolding it, take a sharp knife and trim off any loose bits, or cover the torn corners with the strawberries.

Vanilla sugar is a great way to make use of a leftover vanilla bean half. Add any remaining bean pods to a few cups of sugar and store in an airtight container (or your sugar jar). Let it sit for a week or so for vanilla sugar.

You can roast the berries ahead of time and reheat before serving. They are also great spooned over vanilla ice cream.

○ **KIDS IN THE KITCHEN** ○

Kids of all ages can help butter the molds, measure the ingredients, and scrape out the vanilla bean. They can also toss the strawberries with the vinegar, sugar, and butter. Under supervision, older kids can help unmold the panna cotta, split the vanilla bean, and carefully garnish the plates with the fruit.

CHOCOLATE CANDY CRUNCH

I know there's plenty of great candy out there, but the kids love to make this. Everyone is always shocked when I tell them what provides the crunch: Special K. My Grandma Bea always added a generous handful of my grandfather's cereal to her chocolate chip cookies, and making this reminds me of her. It's delicious on its own or when layered into the ice cream cakes that Mathias and Natasha love to make (see page 147).

1 pound semisweet chocolate, coarsely chopped

1 pound bittersweet chocolate, coarsely chopped

4 tablespoons unsalted butter, cut into pieces

5 cups Special K cereal

SPECIAL EQUIPMENT: minimuffin paper liners or foil candy cups

○ Line a baking sheet with a silicone liner or lightly greased parchment, waxed paper, or foil.

○ Melt the chocolate with the butter in the top of a double boiler, stirring frequently. Or combine in a glass bowl and melt in the microwave, uncovered, for about 1½ to 2 minutes on high. Let cool slightly, and stir in the cereal.

○ Spread out the mixture evenly if using to layer an ice cream cake, or form little clusters or "kisses" that will later fit inside paper or foil candy cups. Set aside at room temperature and let the chocolate harden.

SERVES 6; MAKES ENOUGH FOR ONE LAYER OF 8- TO 9-INCH ROUND CAKE, OR 3 DOZEN INDIVIDUAL CANDY CUPS

NOTE Try substituting Kashi GoLEAN Crunch for the Special K. While candy is certainly not what this healthful cereal was intended for, it makes a sweet treat for special occasions.

VARIATION For Valentine's Day, substitute white chocolate for all the dark chocolate. Form into kisses and sprinkle with red or pink sanding sugar.

○ **KIDS IN THE KITCHEN** ○

Older kids can carefully melt and stir the chocolate and cereal, and fill the cups with the candy, using spoons. Younger kids can spread the cooled crunch onto the ice cream layer.

HOMEMADE ICE CREAM CAKES

A customized ice cream cake doesn't take much effort, and if it's a scorching summer day, you don't even have to turn on the oven. It's also a great project for the kids to help with; they love to decorate, and it gives them a chance to sneak in some candy .

Buy a few quarts of your favorite ice cream in 2 or 3 different flavors. The quantity depends on the crowd and the size of your pan. For a 9-inch springform cake pan, you'll need about 3 quarts. Use the microwave to soften the ice cream slightly, or use the paddle attachment on the stand mixer and beat on low until soft enough to spread.

Spread with one flavor of the ice cream. Layer with the Chocolate Candy Crunch (page 146). Layer with another flavor. Pour over your favorite chocolate sauce, cooled Sour Cream Ganache (page 124), or cooled Toffee Sauce (page 142). We top this with crazy candies. Mathias likes worms and nasty things; Natasha prefers sparkly candies. You may enjoy chopped Toblerone bars. Freeze until serving, for at least 2 hours. Run hot water over a knife, insert between the cake and the pan, and run around the edge of the cake. Remove the sides of the springform, and smooth the edges of the cake if necessary. You can also decorate the sides of the cake.

SERVES 8 TO 10

NOTE You can also make individual cakes by layering into silicone muffin cups.

THINK PINK VALENTINE'S MENUS

Natasha, like many four-year-old girls, is all about pink. Having grown up in a 1970s mod room with an orange, fuchsia, and purple carpet, I'm quite sympathetic and still a fan. Here's a menu for Valentine's or any day that you're feeling blue and should be thinking pink. I use a red onion to add a bit more pink to the Spaghetti Carbonara, my husband's favorite recipe.

- SEARED WRAPPED SCALLOPS WITH BALSAMIC GLAZE (PAGE 43)
- CHINATOWN ROAST PORK (PAGE 71)
- ASIAN RADICCHIO SLAW (PAGE 99)
- SPAGHETTI CARBONARA (PAGE 79)
- PANNA COTTA WITH ROASTED BALSAMIC STRAWBERRIES (PAGE 144)
- POLKA-DOT LINZERTORTE (PAGE 119)
- MERINGUES TINTED WITH PINK FOOD COLORING OR SPRINKLED WITH PINK SUGAR (SEE PAGE 138)
- STRAWBERRY LEMONADE (SEE PAGE 52)

CLOUD PLAYDATE

Whether your kids are the dreamy, head-in-the-clouds type or the rowdier sort, this playdate will engage them all. It's part science lab and part sugar factory. It's a bit sticky and messy, and a lot of fun. Everyone gets to play with fluffy meringue and do a bit of cloud-gazing while the sweets bake, making a lazy way to spend a weekend or late summer afternoon. But switch to a pizza playdate (page 50) if it's humid—meringues tend to weep in wet weather.

There are a few different recipes and techniques for making meringue confections on page 138. Remember to have lots of bowls and a few paper cups set out, so the kids can crack and separate the eggs into two bowls and then transfer the whites to a larger one. That way, one egg with a runny yolk won't ruin the batch. Provide a copper bowl if you have one, and let the kids clean it with a bit of lemon or vinegar to remove any traces of oil, which will prevent the eggs from whipping to their full volume. Offer a big whisk for whipping the egg whites in the copper bowl, as well as a handheld mixer and a stand mixer. If your kids have never whipped whites by hand, race them against the machine. They'll love it.

It's also a good idea to have some plain whites in the fridge, or even a tub of dried egg whites from a baking shop for backup. And no licking fingers. Eating raw egg whites should be avoided. After they've cracked, whipped, learned to fold in cocoa or chocolate chunks or nuts or dried fruits, and piped, dolloped, and decorated, move on to the cloud project below.

CLOUD PROJECT

Make a cloud collage dream book. The kids can draw clouds they see. If it's not a cloudy day, the kids can see clouds on various web sites. Do a search for "clouds." Many universities have pictures online that you can print. If you like, have some photos already printed. You can also have piles of cotton balls and long rolls of cotton to glue on some of the pages, and silver sparkles for the rain showers. Then kids can fill in the clouds with their secret wishes and dreams.

MENU

Nothing here requires your oven, freeing them up for the meringues. The starters and the main courses can be made the day before. Simply reheat the stew on top of the stove, or grill the pre-cooked ribs.

- STUFFED DATES (PAGE 36)
- PICKLED SHRIMP WITH MANGO AND FENNEL (PAGE 47)
- SHORT RIBS WITH CHOCOLATE, ORANGE, AND CINNAMON (PAGES 62–63) OR FRIDGE RIBS (PAGE 70)
- BALSAMIC CHERRY TOMATO SALAD (PAGE 104)
- SNOWBALL SUNDAES AND OTHER MERINGUE DELIGHTS (PAGES 138–139)

CHAPTER 8 | **BREAKFAST ALL DAY**

Breakfast dishes are an ideal blend of flavors and textures—salty, crunchy bacon; sweet fruit; soft, savory eggs with herbs; creamy yogurt; warm toasted bread. I could eat breakfast all day, and in fact we often do. I try to have brunch at our house, or at a friend's, at least once a month.

In the old days we used to have great late-night breakfast parties after hitting a club. Now, serving a midnight supper is not really an option when your kids are up at six a.m., and brunch is a bit of a joke when you start the day that early. So we instituted "backwards day," when we have dessert for breakfast, and invite everyone over for a late-afternoon dinnertime "breakfast."

An array of salty and sweet morning foods can be served all day long, and most can be made ahead, so you aren't standing over the stove flipping eggs when you'd rather be talking to friends and family. If it's a big crowd, pick up extra cartons of your favorite coffee shop–brewed decaf and regular—and fill in with pastries from the local bakery.

COCONUT PANCAKES

While I always keep a stash of whole-grain pancake mix in the pantry out of practical convenience, there are some mornings when we crave these sweet and versatile coconut pancakes. The mango is a refreshing accent, but you can top with any fruit that you have on hand. A few grinds of black pepper and curry powder make these a savory side for a curried stew, and you can make the batter the night before, storing it overnight in the refrigerator. You can also easily halve the recipe.

1¼ cup self-rising cake flour

1 tablespoon sugar

1 egg

1 can coconut milk (14 ounces)

¼ cup milk

4 tablespoons butter

2 tablespoons dark brown sugar

2 mangoes, sliced into moons or chunked

Squeeze of lime

Toasted coconut for garnish

○ In a medium bowl, mix the flour and sugar. In a measuring cup, mix the egg, the coconut milk, and the milk. Using a fork, gently stir the egg mixture into the flour mixture. Do not overmix or the pancakes will become tough. Let the batter sit for about 10–15 minutes while you make the mango topping.

○ In a sauté pan, melt 2 tablespoons of the butter with the brown sugar until bubbling. Add the mango and cook until warmed through. Add a squeeze of lime and a pinch of salt. Set aside.

○ Melt the remaining butter as needed on a griddle or in a skillet, and pour enough batter to make 3-to-4-inch pancakes. Cook over medium-high heat until small bubbles appear on the surface, then flip the pancakes and cook for about 30 seconds more until fully cooked.

○ Keep warm until serving and top with mango and toasted coconut.

SERVES 6

○ **KIDS IN THE KITCHEN** ○

Most children can measure and mix the pancakes. Older kids can learn to trim and cut the mango and help with serving.

BAKER'S DOZEN EGGS

I'm partial to eggs that hit the table with a nice, oozy, golden yolk—poached eggs, eggs *en cocotte,* sunny-side up—but they can be really tricky to cook for a crowd. Believe it or not, you *can* poach eggs in advance and rewarm them later, but the timing can make meeting the school bus on a rainy day look simple. This recipe allows you to cook a dozen or less at the same time. You can prepare the bread baskets the night before. The yolk makes the sauce, but it can be nice to toss a little grated cheese on top, too.

5 tablespoons butter

12 slices extra-thin whole wheat bread (see Notes)

½ pound prosciutto or Serrano ham, thinly sliced

1 dozen large eggs (see Notes)

Kosher salt and freshly ground pepper

¼ cup heavy cream

Chopped fresh chives for garnish

Grated Parmesan or Manchego cheese for garnish

- Preheat the oven to 375 degrees F.

- Butter a 12-cup muffin tin. Butter the bread slices. Press each slice of bread gently into the bottom of a muffin cup. Bake for 3 minutes. (If preparing in advance, allow to cool and wrap the entire muffin tin tightly with foil, then refrigerate.)

- Nestle 1 slice of ham in each bread cup, and carefully crack an egg on top of the ham. Season with salt and pepper, and spoon ½ teaspoon of cream on top of the egg. Carefully place the muffin tin in the oven and bake the eggs for 10 to 15 minutes, until the whites are just set. With an offset spatula, remove the bread cups, transfer to a serving plate, and garnish with chives and cheese. Serve immediately.

SERVES 6, OR 12 AS PART OF A BREAKFAST BUFFET

NOTES If using other bread, either slice very thinly or remove some of the whites.

If you use extra-large or jumbo eggs, you will have to remove some of the whites because they will spill over the muffin tin. Try substituting a thin slice of sausage or Canadian bacon for the ham.

◦ KIDS IN THE KITCHEN ◦

Kids of all ages can help butter the muffin tin and bread, form the cups, add the ham, crack and place the eggs in the muffin tin (with some help), and top with cream, seasonings, and garnishes.

CHORIZO AND SPINACH STRATASPHERE

Stratas are Italian savory bread puddings that need to sit overnight, which makes them very family friendly. They're also incredibly versatile. Keep the milk, egg, and cheese proportions and play around with the fillings—goat cheese with ham or asparagus, Italian sausage and roasted peppers, Gruyère and bacon. I created this Spanish-influenced version with the smoked, dried chorizo I always keep in the fridge. This is oven-to-table cooking, so I like to make it in a rustic ceramic baking dish or a copper gratin dish. You can also make individual stratas in ramekins or ovenproof bowls. Mathias and Natasha like to layer their own; this is just about the only way that they happily eat spinach.

1 large (12- to 14-inch) loaf rustic, crusty bread, or 2 smaller loaves, day old, or lightly toasted

2 teaspoons olive oil

1 pound dried Spanish chorizo or fresh chorizo with casing removed, thinly sliced (see Notes)

1 small onion, or ½ large Spanish onion, chopped

Three 10-ounce packages frozen chopped spinach, thawed and drained well

½ pound Manchego cheese, grated (about 2 ½ to 3 cups)

⅓ pound Parmesan cheese, grated (about 1 cup)

½ teaspoon kosher salt

½ teaspoon freshly ground pepper

4 eggs

1½ cups milk

½ cup heavy cream

1 teaspoon paprika or *pimentón* (Spanish smoked sweet paprika)

○ Preheat the oven to 350 degrees F.

○ Remove the crusts from the bread. (If you do this in big chunks, sprinkle grated cheese on the crusts, and pop under the broiler, for a great snack while you cook!) Slice the bread thinly, no more than ⅓ inch thick.

○ Heat the oil in a large sauté pan over medium-high heat. Add the sausage and cook, stirring occasionally, until slightly crisp, about 1 to 2 minutes. Using a slotted spoon, transfer the sausages to a medium-sized bowl and reserve. Pour off and reserve most of the chorizo oil, leaving about 2 to 3 tablespoons in the pan. Add the onion to the remaining hot oil and sauté until golden brown. Add the spinach to the onions and sauté until any excess water evaporates. The mixture should be fairly dry. Transfer to a bowl with a slotted spoon. Grease a 9-by-13-inch baking dish with a few spoonfuls of the remaining chorizo oil.

○ Cover the bottom of the pan with about a third of the bread in one layer. Top with half of the chorizo. Next, layer with half of the spinach and onion mixture and a third of each cheese. Sprinkle with half of the salt and pepper. Repeat the layers once more, setting aside the remaining cheese. Tear the rest of the bread into large cubes and cover the strata. Gently press the mixture down with your hands.

⊙ In a small bowl, whisk together the eggs, milk, heavy cream, and paprika and pour evenly over the strata. Top with the remaining cheese and drizzle with a bit of the reserved chorizo oil for color and flavor. Cover tightly and refrigerate overnight.

⊙ Remove the strata from the refrigerator, uncover, and let stand at room temperature for 30 minutes. (If you forgot to do this, don't worry; just bake for 15 to 20 minutes longer.)

⊙ Bake for about 1 hour, until the center is set. Cut into large squares and serve.

SERVES 6

NOTES If you are using fresh chorizo, there will be a larger quantity of oil rendered, so drain it carefully, otherwise the strata will be too oily and heavy.

Day-old bread will give you the best texture.

Pimentón, a smoked paprika from Spain, is really worth seeking out. Order it online from La Tienda (see Sources on page 173).

⊙ **KIDS IN THE KITCHEN** ⊙

Older kids can help remove the bread crusts with a serrated knife, under supervision. Most kids can help squeeze the water from the thawed spinach, help remove the sausage from the casing if using fresh sausage, help measure the ingredients, layer the chorizo, spinach, and cheese mixtures (once everything has cooled), crack the eggs, whisk the eggs and milk, pour the custard, and tear the bread.

CHERRY SCONES

These are the infamous scones that I served at my disastrous playdate. Another mother was right in the middle of complaining about how she barely had the time to pick up donuts. When I pulled a tray of hot scones out of the oven, she almost lost it. I tried to explain that scones were really easy, that you could mix the dry ingredients the night before or even throw the finished dough in the freezer a week ahead, but she was never to return. I promise, scones don't take much more time than driving to the donut shop. Plus the kids always like to help with baking. If your guests are new moms, guarantee future playdates by serving only one version at a time (see the variation below).

1¾ cups all-purpose flour

2½ teaspoons baking powder

2½ tablespoons sugar, plus extra for sprinkling on scones

¼ teaspoon salt

6 tablespoons unsalted butter, cut into ½-inch pieces and chilled

½ cup dried cherries

1 teaspoon grated lemon zest

1 egg

5 tablespoons heavy cream, plus extra for brushing on the scones

○ Preheat the oven to 425 degrees F. Line a baking sheet with parchment, waxed paper, or a silicone mat. Set aside.

○ In the bowl of a food processor, combine the flour, baking powder, sugar, and salt. Add the butter and pulse 3 to 6 times until it resembles coarse meal. Transfer the contents to a large bowl. Stir in the dried cherries and lemon zest.

○ In a separate small bowl, beat the egg and cream and add to the flour mixture, stirring gently with a fork until the dough just comes together. It should look like a shaggy mess. You may need to add another splash of cream if the dough seems too dry, but you do not want it to be too sticky.

○ Place the dough on a lightly floured work surface. Gently pat into a 6-inch circle about 1 inch thick. With a sharp knife, divide the dough into 8 equal wedges. Place the scones, without touching, on the prepared baking sheet. Lightly brush the tops with cream and sprinkle with sugar. Bake until golden brown, about 12 to 14 minutes. Serve with jam and butter.

MAKES 8 SCONES

BLUE CHEESE AND DRIED-CHERRY SCONES
Reduce the quantity of sugar to a pinch and omit the lemon zest. Add ½ cup of crumbled blue cheese and ¼ teaspoon of freshly ground pepper along with the dried cherries.

○ **KIDS IN THE KITCHEN** ○

Most kids can measure the ingredients; mix, pat, pulse, and form the dough; brush with cream; and sprinkle with sugar. Older kids can grate the lemon zest and cut the dough into wedges.

WHEN YOU'RE UNDER THE WEATHER

Your head is pounding. Your eyes can barely focus through the excruciating fog of exhaustion and congestion. But the kids don't stop; they just keep on coming. I will not tax your already depleted senses with a precise recipe; this is no time for measuring. Blearily go through your fridge's lower bins, or the supermarket produce aisle if you're unlucky enough to have an empty bin.

In a large pot, halve and juice at least 6 oranges, 2 grapefruits, and 3 lemons. Add the squeezed citrus shells to the pot. Toss in a handful of thyme sprigs and a generous squeeze of honey. If there's still room in the pot, add a splash of OJ or grapefruit juice from the carton. Bring the mixture to a boil, simmer for 10 minutes, and strain, then drink the entire pot. Seriously. Not all at once, but within an hour or so, rewarming as needed. Eat some pound cake or oatmeal if you think your stomach will react poorly to the impending attack of acid and vitamin C. This stuff should put you on the fast track to recovery, so you can get back to your life. Just take it easy. It's the perfect excuse to order in for a couple of days.

HAKUNA (ZUCCHINI) FRITTATA

A cold frittata sandwich with a lemony salad is my idea of heaven. It's summery comfort food and an easy way to make brunch for a crowd without the terrors of individual omelets. This Zucchini Frittata—or Hakuna Frittata, as my kids call it—is fantastic warm, too. I like mine fairly aggressively flavored, so I use Pecorino Romano cheese instead of Parmesan. It's a really flexible and forgiving dish, open to your inspiration. This version includes zucchini and handfuls of basil and mint. You can try adding sautéed cherry tomatoes or eggplant, ribbons of ham, or a mélange of fresh herbs.

¼ cup olive oil

3 cloves garlic, peeled

2 large zucchini, cut lengthwise and thinly sliced into half-moons

8 eggs

½ cup grated Pecorino Romano cheese

¼ teaspoon kosher salt

⅛ teaspoon freshly ground pepper

¼ cup fresh basil leaves, cut into thin ribbons

¼ cup fresh mint leaves, cut into thin ribbons

○ Preheat the broiler.

○ In a 10-inch ovenproof sauté pan over high heat, combine the olive oil and garlic cloves and stir the garlic until the oil shimmers, about 30 seconds. Add the zucchini and sauté, stirring frequently, until they are lightly colored with golden spots, about 4 to 5 minutes.

○ Meanwhile, in a large measuring cup, beat the eggs with the cheese, salt, and pepper. When the zucchini are cooked, remove the garlic cloves, add the herbs, and stir for about 20 seconds. Pour the egg mixture over the herbs. Let the mixture set for a few seconds, as if you were making an omelet. Using a heat-proof spatula, coax the cooked egg mixture away from the sides of the pan into the center, and tilt the pan so some of the liquid runs out, settling around the sides of the pan. Continue doing this until most of the egg has been cooked. The top should look wet and glossy.

○ Remove the pan from the heat and place under the broiler for 1 minute or so, until the top is browned and puffy. Slide the frittata onto a serving plate; cut into wedges; and serve hot, at room temperature, or cold.

SERVES 4 TO 6

MIDNIGHT SUPPER OR SLUMBER PLAYDATE

Slumber parties or just late-night silliness when everyone wears pajamas are always fun during a summer night spent stargazing, or as a way to brighten up one of those endless gray winter weekends. We love to rustle up a "midnight" breakfast at six o'clock. Put the kids to work mixing up batches of scones, with different dried fruits or even chocolate chips. Or set up assembly lines to make the Baker's Dozen Eggs (page 155) in muffin tins, or Stuffed French Toast (page 162). Have a smoothie bar with assorted fresh fruit or bags of frozen fruit (which is a lot less work). The kids can also make colored sugar (see page 170) to serve alongside coffee and non-caffeinated fruit teas.

My kids love to "sew" and decorate goofy, old-fashioned sleeping caps out of felt triangles and yarn. Just pick up large felt squares, yarn, and needles with large eyes at a craft shop, as well as extra glue, glitter (if you can stand it), pompoms, and trimmings. For younger kids, you can glue the hats together, though they won't hold up as long.

Or you can go more upscale and make spa treatments. Pick up plain bath salts at the drugstore, and mix them in with dried lavender or rosemary. You can make scrubs with kosher salt, honey, and lemon rind, or substitute oatmeal for the salt. Pack into plastic containers and decorate the labels.

STUFFED FRENCH TOAST

These stuffed toasts are designed to feed a crowd while keeping things personal with custom fillings. The kids enjoy creating their own fillings and the assembly line action of stuffing the sandwiches. Or you can cook a bunch of this savory dish and its sweet variation ahead of time and rewarm them when your friends arrive. Be creative. Try goat cheese and tapenade, or cream cheese and smoked salmon with dill, or, for the sweet version top the mascarpone with peaches or apricots sprinkled with brown sugar. Serve the sandwiches cut in half so everyone can try a few. You can easily halve or double the recipe, depending on the size of the crowd.

6 slices brioche or white bread, 1 inch thick

2 tablespoons Dijon mustard

6 thin slices sweet soppressata or ham

6 thin slices provolone cheese (see Notes)

6 eggs

1¼ cups milk

Pinch of kosher salt

Freshly ground black pepper

3 tablespoons unsalted butter

3 tablespoons neutral oil, such as canola or grapeseed

Confectioners' sugar and/or maple syrup (preferably grade B) for serving

○ Preheat the oven to 350 degrees F.

○ Starting at the top of the bread slice, make a slit almost to the bottom, but do not cut all the way through the bread. The piece should look like an open book.

○ Spread some of the mustard on one side of the bread, tuck a slice of ham and cheese inside, and close the sandwich. Repeat with the remaining bread.

○ Combine the eggs, milk, salt, and pepper in a shallow rectangular baking dish, about 9 by 13 inches. Whisk to blend.

○ Place the stuffed breads in the egg mixture and leave for about 1 minute. Turn and leave in the mixture for another 1 minute.

○ In a large sauté pan over medium to high heat, combine 1 tablespoon of the butter and 1 tablespoon of the oil and swirl to coat the base of the pan. When the butter is bubbling, add 2 of the stuffed toasts and cook for about 2 minutes until golden brown. Turn and cook for another minute or so until golden. Remove from the pan and transfer to a baking sheet. Repeat with the remaining butter, oil, and stuffed breads.

○ Place the baking sheet in the oven and bake the stuffed breads for 10 minutes, or until the cheese is melting. Cut in half on the diagonal, and top with a sprinkle of confectioners' sugar or a drizzle of syrup.

SERVES 6

NOTES Use aged provolone instead of regular for a sharper flavor.

These toasts can be assembled the night before, or even sautéed hours ahead and stored in the fridge. Finish in the oven when everyone arrives.

○ **KIDS IN THE KITCHEN** ○

Older kids can help slice the bread and sauté the toasts. Younger ones can help fill the toasts, measure the ingredients, crack the eggs, combine the eggs and milk, soak the stuffed toasts, and top with sugar or syrup.

SWEET STUFFED FRENCH TOAST

Replace the mustard, ham, and cheese with ¼ pound mascarpone cheese, 2 tablespoons of dark brown sugar or honey, and ½ pint of raspberries. Slice the bread as instructed above. Spread one side of the bread with the mascarpone, sprinkle with brown sugar or drizzle with honey, top with berries, and close. Make the egg mixture, omitting the pepper, and proceed with the recipe.

SUGAR-AND-SPICE BACON

I don't think breakfast is complete without bacon, and the crispy coating of brown sugar and cayenne here hits just the right note. I usually make a third of the batch without the cayenne for the kids. These are great on turkey burgers and a must-have at the birthday Burger Bar (see page 68). Natasha likes to curl these into little rosettes before baking while Mathias prefers to twist them like cheese sticks for a fancier garnish.

1 pound bacon

1 cup brown sugar, light or dark

½ teaspoon cayenne, or more to taste

○ Preheat the oven to 400 degrees F.

○ Place a baking rack over a foil-lined baking sheet and place the bacon across the rack. Sprinkle the sugar and cayenne over both sides of the bacon. Bake for 15 minutes, or until crispy. Drain on paper towels and serve immediately.

SERVES 6

NOTE Slightly underbake the bacon if preparing in advance and rewarm at 350 degrees F for 5 or so minutes before serving.

○ KIDS IN THE KITCHEN ○

Kids of all ages can help sugar the bacon and curl it into rosettes or twist it like breadsticks.

BANANABERRY SMOOTHIES

I've met plenty of kids who just don't "do" fruit but happily down smoothies, to the relief of exasperated parents. Mathias and Natasha like to plunk the frozen berries and yogurt in the blender and drizzle in different honeys that we collect. An offbeat juice helps give the smoothie its zing. The measurements don't need to be precise. I suggest using low-fat organic yogurts, which don't have all the added sugars.

1 cup fresh or frozen berries (see Note)

1 cup plain low-fat yogurt

1 banana

1 generous teaspoon honey

¼ to ½ cup guava, apricot, or passion fruit juice

Banana or pineapple slices for garnish

SPECIAL EQUIPMENT: colorful straws for serving

Combine all the ingredients in the jar of the blender. Blend, adding extra juice as needed to thin for easy pouring. Pour into glasses, garnish each glass with a slice of fruit, and tuck in a straw.

SERVES 2 TO 4

NOTE Frozen berries allow us to enjoy smoothies year-round. If using fresh berries, add about a ¼ cup of ice cubes to the blender before blending.

For safety, omit the honey for children under the age of one.

POMPOM

Tired of the typical mimosa? Try switching to Italian Prosecco, a slightly sweet bubbly wine. Pour into tall narrow glasses or Champagne flutes and add a splash of pomegranate juice and a few fresh pomegranate seeds to each drink. For the kids, pour a splash of pomegranate juice over their orange juice so they can watch it float.

○ KIDS IN THE KITCHEN ○

Kids can add all of the ingredients to the blender, push buttons while being supervised, help pour, garnish, and serve. Older kids can slice the fruit for garnish.

POTATO PANCAKES WITH BACON AND CHEESE

Crispy, buttery potatoes stuffed with salty bacon and cheese—all that goodness in one dish. These pancakes are crowd-pleasing comfort food. They dress up plain eggs, and are assertive enough to accompany eggs scrambled with peppers. My friend, chef Jeff Mora (who feeds the Los Angeles Lakers), taught me the trick of cooking the potatoes the night before to deliver the best texture. It's the kind of tip that I really appreciate the morning of a big brunch. The fillings are limited only by your imagination, so experiment. Jeff likes to fill his with fancy Gruyère and sautéed leeks, but you could add sautéed mushrooms and Fontina, or try Natasha's favorite—layer savory smoked salmon inside and dab a bit of sour cream and dill sprigs on top. These are also fun to serve mini-sized for a fall or winter soirée.

6 large russet potatoes

¼ cup kosher salt

Freshly ground pepper

6 tablespoons unsalted butter

2 scallions, thinly sliced

4 slices bacon, cooked and crumbled

4 tablespoons olive or canola oil

¼ pound cheddar or Monterey Jack cheese, grated

○ Put the potatoes in a large pot of cold water to cover and add the ¼ cup of kosher salt to the pot. Slowly bring to a boil, then reduce the heat and simmer the potatoes until tender, about 15 to 20 minutes. Drain and let cool. Refrigerate the potatoes overnight.

○ The following day, peel the potatoes and grate into a bowl. Season to taste with salt and pepper, and set aside. Heat 2 tablespoons of the butter in a medium sauté pan over medium-high heat. Add the scallions and sauté until tender, about 3 to 5 minutes. Transfer to a bowl, add the crumbled bacon, and set aside.

○ Preheat the oven to 300 degrees F.

○ To make the pancakes, combine 2 tablespoons of the butter and 2 tablespoons of the oil in a medium nonstick sauté pan and heat over medium-high heat. Add a quarter of the potatoes and spread out evenly in the pan. Top with half of the scallion and bacon mixture and half of the cheese. Cover evenly with another quarter of the potatoes and press down with a spatula. Brown the potatoes for about 5 minutes. Place a plate over the top. Flip the pancake over and slide it back into the pan. Brown for another 5 minutes. Transfer to an ovenproof platter or baking sheet, and place in the oven to keep warm. Repeat for the second pancake.

○ Cut the pancakes into wedges and serve.

SERVES 6

○ KIDS IN THE KITCHEN ○

Older kids can peel the cold potatoes and carefully grate the potatoes and cheese under supervision. They can also cut the pancakes into wedges with either a knife or kitchen scissors under supervision.

FAVORS AND GIFTS

I always keep rolls of cellophane and colored tissue paper, instead of wrapping paper, to wrap gifts and form little bundles of treats to give away. Cut large squares, pull up the corners, and tie like a big beggar's purse. Or cut a large rectangle and wrap rectangular things like breads or a cardboard tube the kids have decorated and filled with cookies. Tie like a big tootsie roll at each end. It's festive and easy for birthday party favor bags, holiday treats, or when you're rushed, like I usually am.

THE MUST-HAVES

- JUMBO ROLLS OF CELLOPHANE PAPER, CLEAR AND COLORED
- COLORED TISSUE PAPER
- RIBBON
- CELLOPHANE BAGS
- BROWN PAPER LUNCH BAGS
- DECORATIVE SCISSORS
- PLAIN STICKERS

PLAYDATE PANTRY

I believe that your pantry should do at least half of the work for you. Whether it's one crowded shelf, or a customized, gorgeous, handcrafted room, if you have the provisions you need, you can have fun. Having a well stocked pantry is my security blanket. It means less running to the store, and no fear of last-minute plans.

I've listed some of my favorite purchased specialty foods that can be served straight from the jar, and some beauties that can easily transform the most basic ingredients into an impressive meal. An array of flavored oils and vinegars, spices, and spice blends transform everything from hummus to ice cream.

Here are some suggestions in alphabetical order. See Sources (page 173) for details.

CANDIED COLORED SUGARS I buy these on sale after the holidays and keep a variety to decorate cookies, cakes, and rims of glasses. You can also make your own, which is fun for the kids. Dip a toothpick into food coloring paste and stir into a small bowl of sugar. Not as precise, but it will do in a pinch.

CHICKEN STOCK I do try to make my own stock, but I don't always have the time or the room in the fridge. I prefer Swanson's stock and Knorr stock cubes.

CHOCOLATE Milk, semisweet, bittersweet, white, custom-blended—the choices are incredible. The best way to decide which chocolate you prefer is, well, by eating. Many Web sites like www.chocosphere.com offer chocolate tasting guides. Alice Medrich has written many a fine book explaining all of the different uses along with recipes. French pastry chef extraordinaire Pierre Hermé introduced me to one of my favorites, Valrhona Manjari. Buy the best available that you can afford, and consider your audience.

COCOA POWDER A richly flavored "gourmet" or imported cocoa powder from Valrhona or Scharffen Berger and organic from Dagoba add deep chocolate flavors.

COCONUT MILK Stir into chicken soup with curry paste, or into leftover chicken and veggies. Or use for rice pudding or a dessert risotto, or for Coconut Pancakes (page 153).

CONDIMENTS I always buy pickles, chutneys, relishes, and jams and jellies when I travel. Then I torture Anthony by packing them in the corners of the suitcase. A little dish of Texan pickled okra or Spanish roasted piquillo peppers fill out a quick cheese plate. My friend Rick Field makes incredible wasabi string beans and a variety of "Rick's Picks." In Northern California, I discovered that anything June Taylor or Robert Lambert makes (such as June's Meyer Lemon Jam, and Robert's dessert syrups) will transform whatever they touch. I'm also partial to Italian Agrimontana Sour Cherry Jam.

CRACKERS I am always hunting for a new cracker to add to my stock of Carr's, Finn Rye Caraway, thick multigrain Wasa, Asian rice crackers, and fennel semolina raisin toasts. I recently discovered wafer-thin Australian Water Wheels, available from igourmet.com.

DRIED FRUIT The snack of choice in our house. I always have dried apples, apricots, raisins, currants, cherries, strawberries, figs, and dates to toss into cooked rice, pasta salads, and tossed salads. (I skip the blueberries because Mathias is allergic.) My grandmother always kept a small tray of Turkish figs and apricots and a bowl of pistachios on the coffee table to welcome visitors, a tradition we continue.

DRIED NUTS See From the Freezer (page 75).

DRIED PASTA DeCecco is widely available and reliable. I pick up whatever looks intriguing, and have been happy with Latini and Cipriani, as well.

FLOUR I have a shelf of flour containers that are clearly labeled. I stock a variety King Arthur flours for baking and cooking, as well as cake flour, and self-rising cake flour. This flour already includes baking soda and salt, and is typically used in Southern and British baking. I find this makes things go faster, one less thing to fumble for with a measuring spoon. If the recipe calls for it and you don't have it, simply add 1½ teaspoons of baking powder and ½ teaspoon of salt to 1 cup of all-purpose flour.

GRAINS In addition to dried pasta and couscous, dried wheat berries, buckwheat, and quinoa are good to have on hand to add some texture and richness to leftovers or make a side dish. Cook the grain(s) according to package directions, then toss them with leftover chopped chicken or steak, along with some chopped bell peppers and herbs, and dress like a salad with lime juice and extra-virgin olive oil. Quinoa cooks the fastest. Mix it with chopped peppers and cold chicken or leftover grilled steak, and dress like a salad with lime and oil.

HONEY While the sweet squeeze bear certainly has a proud place in my pantry, I also have half a dozen other honeys keeping him company. These are special varieties that we collect from health food or specialty stores, or pick up when we travel. Dark Italian chestnut, fragrant French lavender, aromatic Tasmanian eucalyptus from Australia, or rare tropical honey from Maui can be drizzled on roast pork loins. American Savannah Bee honey mixed with mustard is good on chicken breasts or tossed with nuts before roasting for a nibble. Visit local honey farms or individual beekeepers who give tours and bring home some fresh honeycomb; it makes a novel way to dress up a cheese platter.

MAYONNAISE Hellmann's or Best Foods work well for most things, and I love the fresh Delouis et Fils mayonnaise and aioli for crudités. You may find it in the refrigerator section of your local specialty market.

MUSTARD I am addicted to Edmund Fallot Dijon, both the regular and coarse. When we were in Dijon, I horrified Anthony by trying to bribe the owners into letting me have a factory tour. It didn't work, but I still adore it. For hot dogs it's always my brother's restaurant brand, Artie's Deli.

OILS AND VINEGARS I constantly try new ones, and I have a range on hand. For regular olive oil, I often buy Spanish or Greek. For basic extra virgin oil, I like San Giuliano, which many supermarkets carry, and oils from small California companies, like the full and fruity Pasolivo or any of the peppery ones like DaVero. I also like the Spanish oils made with arbequina olives. A splash of flavored oils (orange, lemon, or herb) is an easy way to invigorate store-bought spreads or last-minute salads. Drizzle over sliced roast meats or fish. I avoid the ones with garlic as they turn rancid too quickly. Agrumato actually presses the olives and the lemons together for an incredible oil. The best way to buy is to try and taste at a specialty market, or purchase from a trusted Web site (see Sources, page 173). My pantry also holds flavored fruit vinegars like grapefruit or fig, imported Spanish sherry vinegar, and Champagne, American cider, everyday balsamic, and aged balsamic vinegars.

OLIVES It's relatively easy to find good olives, but you can always rinse the standard supermarket variety and toss with warm olive oil, citrus rind, and pepper flakes. Serve them right away, or let them marinate for a few days in the refrigerator.

SALT Although I have a little basket filled with many different salts, I always cook with kosher salt and tend to garnish with British Maldon sea salt, which crumbles nicely between your fingers. My mom brings us salt from her vacations—flavored and smoked from Maine, and gray from France. I like to explain to the kids how the salt is harvested and have them taste the difference with small steamed potatoes or on a bit of bread and butter. Pink salt from Hawaii looks beautiful alongside radishes and a ramekin of cold butter, and I recently saw a hunk of pink Himalayan Salt that is sold with a grater.

SPICES Whenever possible, I buy in bulk from Penzeys, Vann's, or the Spice Hunter, and I pick up intriguing blends when I travel or stop at specialty stores. They make instant rubs or marinades, and can be added to hummus dips or vinaigrettes. And I always have La Chinata–brand sweet *pimentón*, the Spanish smoked paprika that I add to everything from leftover chicken salad to roast potatoes.

SOURCES

INGREDIENTS

ARTIE'S DELI
2290 Broadway
New York, NY 10024
www.arties.com
Deli mustard, pastrami in a box

CHOCOSPHERE
www.chocosphere.com
Every chocolate and cocoa powder imaginable

COWGIRL CREAMERY
80 Fourth Street
Point Reyes Station, CA 94956
mailorder@cowgirlcreamery.com
Phone: 866.433.7834 (toll-free); 415.663.9335

D'ARTAGNAN
www.dartagnan.com
Phone: 800.327.8246
Duck, demi-glace, pâté, foie gras, and more

IGOURMET
www.igourmet.com
Phone: 877.IGOURMET
Edmund Fallot mustard, honeys, specialty items

JUNE TAYLOR COMPANY
The Still-Room
2207 4th Street
Berkeley, CA 94710
info@junetaylorjams.com
Phone: 510.548.2236

KALUSTYAN'S
123 Lexington Avenue
New York, NY 10016
www.kalustyans.com
Phone: 212.685.3451
Black mustard seeds, curry powders, rices

LA TIENDA
www.tienda.com
Phone: 888.472.1022
All things Spanish: chorizo, pimentón, oils, marcona almonds, and more

MAYTAG DAIRY FARMS
www.maytagdairyfarms.com
Phone: 800.247.2458

MURRAY'S CHEESE SHOP
257 Bleecker Street
New York, NY 10014
www.murrayscheese.com
Phone: 888.MYCHEEZ

RICK'S PICKS
www.rickspicksnyc.com
Award winning pickles and more

ROBERT LAMBERT
www.robertlambert.com
Phone: 415.256.8110
Dessert sauces, fruit syrups, and more

ZINGERMAN'S DELICATESSEN
620 Phoenix Drive
Ann Arbor, MI 48108
www.zingermans.com
Phone: 888.636.8162
Smart selection of olive oils and vinegars, cheeses, condiments, specialty items

EQUIPMENT AND TABLETOP

ATECO
www.atecousa.com
Phone: 800.645.7170
Spatulas, cookie cutters, baking supplies

BRIDGE KITCHENWARE
711 Third Avenue
New York, NY 10022
www.bridgekitchenware.com
Phone: 800.274.3435

CHEFWEAR
www.chefwear.com
Phone: 800.568.2433
Aprons, chefs' coats, and pants for kids and adults

CLIO
92 Thompson Street
New York, NY 10012
www.clio-home.com
Phone: 212.966.8991
Amazing tabletop treasures

CRATE & BARREL
www.crateandbarrel.com

DEADLY SQUIRE
www.deadlysquire.com
Inventive aprons, pot holders, and decorative pillows

JOHN ROBSHAW
www.johnrobshaw.com
Linens, napkins, and decorative pillows

THE KNIFE MERCHANT
www.knifemerchant.com
Ludwig Schiff knives

MISSONI
Tea set and tabletop items available at Barneys and Macy's department stores

MUD AUSTRALIA
www.mudaustralia.com
Pottery, serving pieces

SAMBONET
www.sambonet.it
sales@sambonetusa.com
Phone: 800.887.4863
Gio Ponti flatware, Paderno pots

SUR LA TABLE
www.surlatable.com
Phone: 800.243.0852

WILLIAMS-SONOMA
www.williams-sonoma.com
Phone: 877.812.6235

WILTON CAKE
www.wilton.com
Cake decorating and baking equipment

SILICONE

www.laprimashops.com

www.siliconezone.com

www.surlatable.com

www.williams-sonoma.com

NUTRITIONAL WEBSITES

www.darwindeen.com

www.lisahark.com

www.5aday.gov

www.foodpolitics.com
(Dr. Marion Nestle's website)

www.exploratorium.edu/cooking

ACKNOWLEDGMENTS

This book represents a journey from my childhood kitchen table through cooking school into the television world and back to my own children's kitchen table. Many people inspired and supported me along the way, and I am incredibly grateful that they have taken part in this playdate.

My parents, Susan Bank and Ronald Bank, made our kitchen a lively place filled with exciting food and exotic cookbooks. I remember visiting the original Dean & DeLuca, in the late 1970s, with the same awe accorded to the surrounding SoHo galleries. My grandmothers, Beatrice Bank and Sylvia Sachs Page, were very different cooks, but both set the warmest, magical tables. My aunt and uncle, Linda and Roger Bank, continue to share their generosity, spirit, and culinary memories that helped me reproduce some of the lost family recipes included here.

My brother and sister-in-law, Jeffrey and Karen Bank, allowed me to invade their weekend house countless times during crucial development and testing periods, when it turned out our temporary rental had a closet for a kitchen; and my niece Sarah and nephew Andrew were incredibly patient and donned pajamas for hours on end for the photo shoot. And many thanks to Jane Spath Bank and Irene Deen for their continuous support.

This book would still be a half-written proposal if not for my agent, Angela Miller, who steered these pages away from its original idea—a compilation of chefs' recipes—into my own baby, and for that I am quite grateful.

Bill LeBlond immediately embraced the idea of Kitchen Playdates, and has been an exceptional editor and perfect partner for a first-time author. Amy Treadwell, fellow working mom and talented associate editor, deserves a promotion for all of her efforts! The entire team at Chronicle is remarkable, especially Peter Perez, Vanessa Dina, Doug Ogan, Evan Hulka, Steve Kim, and Jennifer Tomaro.

The collaborative efforts of what I think of as my home team made this book really come to life, and I couldn't have done this without Henry Tenney, writer and star producer, who read every word and, when necessary, untangled my twisted prose into funny and smart moments, much like himself. My photographer, Tina Rupp, is truly a dream—smart, talented, creative, and able to remain calm while helping me adjust from the crazy TV world to her still one, shooting amid moving trucks and children and dogs. Deborah Williams shopped, schlepped, and became a dear friend while adding style to the shots with every plate, napkin, and odd treasure she unearthed. A special thank-you to Toni Brogan, who added her artistry and insight to the food; Holly Moore, who tested, tasted, and organized the recipes; as well as Andrea Albin, for helping me to the finish line. Television dynamos and stellar parents Meredith Bennett and Robert LaForty graciously shared their home and their adorable sons, Colin and Ryan, for a very long shoot day.

My chef friends shared more than just their recipes, and I am indebted to Jimmy Bradley, who makes the Red Cat feel like our living room; Lee Hanson, fellow parent and true talent; and Jeffrey Mora, who has more ideas and energy than those L.A. Lakers he feeds. A very special thank-you to Bobby Flay, who took a chance on a young producer and let me lure him away from the Food Network for a brief moment more than 10 years ago. He shared more than just a recipe for these pages—he also shared the importance of being a parent and not only a producer.

Martha Stewart provided me the experience of a lifetime, the opportunity to "learn something new every day" from an incredible woman who has changed the way we view the home arts and the skills of everyday artisans.

Many friends ate, retested recipes, and listened to my whining, while balancing their own families and careers, and for that I am forever grateful: especially to Beverly Ellar Self, a most remarkable and inspiring woman (and talented producer), and all the Croton moms for their encouragement and house parties—Deborah Polansky Schor, Julie Spedialere, and especially my partner in crime, Sarah Murphy—who helped me push Kitchen Playdates forward in new ways.

Hurray for all the Brooklyn parents from P.S. 58 as well as the staff—Principal Giselle Gault, Alice Zundos, and Ms. Marsh and the PTA—who let me work out many of the concepts for this book in class, with a special note for the patience and friendship of Angus Killick, Michael Yuen, Theo Killick-Yuen, Sharon Tang and Jason Wong, Denise Figlar Wilson, Liam and Ella Wilson, and Donna Louch and the adorable Finley, who all braved photo shoots in our day-old apartment.

Anya von Bremzen, cookbook author extraordinaire, has provided years of fabulous friendship, dinner parties, and a keen editor's eye, plus a delicious recipe for the book. New mom Pamela Cannon offered hours of advice and encouragement, while birthing a new business and baby.

My best friend Betsy Krebs has inspired and challenged me, letting me tag along to Madrid back in 1987, where I threw my first crazy dinner party, and has been a true friend for the hundreds of parties ever since, along with her husband, Sheldon, and those delicious kids, Gabriel and Daisy. Hay tortilla!

More than 18 years ago I tripped over Anthony Deen on a movie set (literally), and it was only with his love, focus, unwavering support, and wry humor that I was able to quit what most thought was the best job in the world and discover what the best job in the world really is for me. This book is for him, and for our children, Mathias and Natasha, who are the best playdate in town. Oh, and for Nikolai, the wonder dog, too.

INDEX

TABLE OF EQUIVALENTS

The exact equivalents in the following tables have been rounded for convenience.

LIQUID/DRY MEASURES

U.S.	METRIC	
¼ teaspoon	1.25	milliliters
½ teaspoon	2.5	milliliters
1 teaspoon	5	milliliters
1 tablespoon (3 teaspoons)	15	milliliters
1 fluid ounce (2 tablespoons)	30	milliliters
¼ cup	60	milliliters
⅓ cup	80	milliliters
½ cup	120	milliliters
1 cup	240	milliliters
1 pint (2 cups)	480	milliliters
1 quart (4 cups, 32 ounces)	960	milliliters
1 gallon (4 quarts)	3.84	liters
1 ounce (by weight)	28	grams
1 pound	454	grams
2.2 pounds	1	kilogram

LENGTHS

U.S.	METRIC	
⅛ inch	3	millimeters
¼ inch	6	millimeters
½ inch	12	millimeters
1 inch	2.5	centimeters

OVEN TEMPERATURES

FAHRENHEIT	CELSIUS	GAS
250	120	½
275	140	1
300	150	2
325	160	3
350	180	4
375	190	5
400	200	6
425	220	7
450	230	8
475	240	9
500	260	10